POWER IN MIDLIFE AND BEYOND

Peace & Blessings,
Dr. Barbara

Power in Midlife and Beyond: 14 Tips to Create an

Authentic Life©

Dr. Barbara R. Collins

ISBN - 978-1-4951-0454-1

1533017999

Printed in the United States of America

POWER IN MIDLIFE AND BEYOND:

14 TIPS TO CREATE AN AUTHENTIC LIFE

by Dr. Barbara R. Collins

Copyright © 2014

All Rights Reserved

PUBLISHED BY:

Dr. Barbara Collins
www.drbarbaracollins.com

Dedicated to Sherri's Memory

FOREWORD

There's no reason for a mid-life crisis in mid-life!

Dr. Barbara Collins is testimony to that. I've known Barbara for more than 20 years – professionally and personally. I've always admired her courage, her strength, and her creativity.

Her life, like most of ours, has not always been smooth. Throughout her diverse experiences and during many challenging times, she's discovered ways that have helped her feel healthier and have pleasure in life. Now she is sharing them with the rest of us!

I've personally seen women fall into two categories: "Oh no I'm older; I have nothing to look forward to." And those that are just naturally optimistic and excited about discovering new things.

Which one are you?

If you're a naysayer, then this book will help you see the possibilities. Barbara's use of homework assignments will keep you accountable to change your mindset and behavior.

If you're already a glass half-full person, then she will reinforce your optimistic outlook and natural strengths – providing 14 chapters of "Funthentic" tips that are fun and exciting to help you begin your journey in rediscovering your authentic self."

So, buckle up, and get ready to embark on your new adventure – to discover your *Power in Mid-life and Beyond*.

Marjorie Brody, CSP, PCC, CPAE Speaker Hall of Fame, and CEO, BRODY Professional Development

ACKNOWLEDGEMENTS

I want to thank all the women who enjoyed reading my first book, *It's Your Turn: Find Your Authentic Self and go Fetch It!* Many women attended my *"It's Your Turn"* seminars and keynote presentations. Women from all occupations, race, socio-economic levels, occupation and education shared powerful stories at the seminars about their journey to self-discovery. I'm humbly grateful for the courage and willingness women demonstrated in my seminars to find power in midlife and beyond.

Women sent numerous emails asking for more activities to rediscover authentic and natural strengths. *Power in Midlife and Beyond: 14 Tips to Create an Authentic Life* was written to include more tips and learn how living an authentic life gives you power in midlife and beyond.

I learned a lot about the women in midlife and beyond who dared to share their passion, pain and dreams about getting older. If you attended any of my seminars, where ever you are – I wish you peace and a life celebrating who you really are.

An African proverb says it takes a village to raise a child; well it also takes friends, professionals, and family to sometimes achieve a goal or follow your dreams. These people are my "personal board of directors." I think we all deserve a "personal board of directors." I think this could be another book.

Thank you to my editor, Lorraine Castle "Castle Virtual Solutions, LLC." Her valuable editing and publishing expertise is a treasure. Her patience, detailed and organized skills were immensely helpful in completing the last phase of my book. The bonus meeting Lorraine was finding out that Lorraine was located in another state close to Pennsylvania and she is a Christian.   I discovered Lorraine by connecting to the IVAA, International Virtual Assistant Association website. The IVAA was instrumental in learning about the virtual assistant hiring process. I was truly impressed.

Erin Hyland, my web manager, provided invaluable expertise with social media. She is also my accountability manager for making sure I complete my tasks in creating my new Blog and refreshing my web site. Not only is Erin technically astute she motivated and encouraged me to keep following my dream,

I am grateful that Marjorie Brody agreed to write the forward for my book. We both share a long association as friends and members in the National Speakers Association.   Her success in delivering training and coaching for 30 years has been an inspiration to me. I can always reach out to Marjorie for advice and catching up on our current business endeavors.

There are a special group of women I must thank, Doris Hanna, Connie Rose, Jo Ann Jolivet, Everene Johnson, and Carole Copland Thomas. These women took time in their busy schedules to read the manuscript and offer poignant suggestions. Words of appreciation to my dear friend and Soror, Joyce Finch, Baugh for suggesting women from her book club to preview the manuscript. Thanks Joyce!

My family and friends always see in me more than I see in myself. Too many to name but they know who they are! My daughters – Monique Moore Pryor, Esq. and Sherri Moore give me strength and encouragement in all my endeavors. Watching them grow into beautiful, strong and amazing women has always been my impetus to show up each day to follow my life's purpose. Mecca and Micah, my granddaughters; talking about these girls could turn into another book! They are beautiful, smart and talented. Yes, sorry I'm a typical grand mom with bragging rights! Mecca and Micah remind me to stay in the present moment and enjoy what is most important.

My life partner Ben, continues to be my biggest fan. I thank him from the bottom of my heart for believing in me and supporting me in my dreams. We do make a great team!

As an active member of the National Speakers Association (NSA), I continue to learn insights about the professional speaking business by attending local chapter meetings with NSA-PHL.

My authentic journey is embedded in my love of God through Christ. It always amazes me that when I turn to God in faith his wisdom and plan always comes right on time. He shaped me to be who I am. I knew from the beginning that I did not come into this world with a blank slate of skills and talents. When doubts and hurdles appeared while writing my book, the Spirit of God was always with me, showing me who I am. God continues to work on me – as they say I am a work in progress.

I am grateful for completing *Power in Midlife and Beyond: 14 Tips to Create an Authentic Life.*

To my readers.

Thank you for reading my book!

REVIEWS AND TESTIMONIES

"I found myself nodding in agreement as I read the manuscript, *Power In Midlife and Beyond.* Dr. Collins provides validation that we should not confine and/or define ourselves by our past professional accomplishments. Instead, midlife can be a time to acknowledge what we have to offer, to explore our dormant talents and do those things we wanted to try but did not have the time, confidence or courage to interject into our busy professional and family life. By the time we reach midlife and beyond, we may have 'been there and done that,' but there is still more beyond the horizon. I pledge to be 'authentic.'"

> Jo Ann C. Jolivet
> jcjvet@starpower.net or joannjolivet@yahoo.com

"Midlife, a time of restlessness and discontent, is a much researched topic but very little day-to-day/step-by-step practices for empowered navigation has been written. Dr. Barbara R. Collins blends scientific research with philosophical teachings to create a doable practical manual designed to address and conquer the 'challenges of midlife that can become a force that shakes our inner core.'

I find the book to be an authentic tool to use to confront the present with an eye on managing and planning for an enjoyable future."

> Everene Johnson-Turner
> Consultant at Forever55 LLC

"I believe your book can energize and motivate women as they seek and understand their authentic selves. The ways in which they can be leaders, work and live with really will be more meaningful because of your sharing your own life experiences and successes.

The Funthentic Tips are laid out so that women of all ages can use them or adapt them to their lives to lead them to a more meaningful, productive, fulfilling, and happy life.

I have granddaughters and nieces who I know will benefit from your book when it is published.

Be blessed."

> Doris Hanna
> The Society, Inc.

"*Power In Midlife and Beyond* is a remarkable demonstration of creating a purpose-filled life. Barbara artfully weaves in her real life stories with substantial resources and clinical research that illuminate her points. It's a straightforward, simple yet elegantly written guide to living authentically no matter where life takes you. From her days on public assistance to receiving her doctorate and working in the financial services industry, Barbara's real life story and her 14 Funthentic Tips are an inspiration for anyone looking to leverage every opportunity to succeed in life."

> Carole Copeland Thomas, MBA, CDMP
> Global Diversity Professional
> Multicultural Symposium Series
> www.tellcarole.com

"Barbara shares her life experiences so that her readers can benefit from them. For me, the best part of her book is her 14 "Funthentic" tips. Readers get specific tools to help them create the life they choose to live in midlife. Barbara's a great teacher!"

Connie Rose
Leadership and Career Coach
C. Rose Coaching
www.coachconnie.com

Contents

My New Story

My life changed on July 5, 2014 when my daughter Sherri, at age 49, went on to her new home with God. Sherri lost her battle with breast cancer that led to terminal brain cancer. A month later I had a hemorrhagic stroke.

It's been over a year-and-a-half since Sherri transitioned and the stroke. It's a miracle that I recovered quickly from the stroke. My doctor told me that this type of stroke could have been fatal. His prognosis was to be happy. I knew I would never be the same after surviving a near fatal health challenge and losing my daughter. This is my testimony about how God's grace and mercy lifted my inner spiritual power during this difficult time.

Each day the burden of grief is unexplainable. Feeling the loss of my daughter, at times, is overwhelming. Grief feels like an emotional roller coaster that comes in waves when you least expect it. Sometimes these feelings take my breath, and I have to pause and let the feelings pass. Melody Beattie, author of *"More Language of Letting Go,"* who lost a child describes my feelings best. She says, "To the untrained, casual eye, each wave looks the same. It is not. No two are the same. And each one washes away the old, and washes in the new." I have flash backs in the hospital watching Sherri battle the cancer with courage. I embrace these feelings with compassion. The supernatural experiences from God's grace and mercy in the hospital remind me that all is Divine. My family and friends sustain me when my resolve is low.

Why add this chapter to my book? There are two main reasons.

My second book *"Power in Midlife and Beyond"* was completed two months prior to Sherri's transition. Reverend Demett Jenkins was always by Sherri's side supporting her in whatever she needed spiritually. One day, Reverend Demett invited me to sit with her in the garden to talk about what support I needed for me and my family. We talked about faith, courage and my belief in God. I told her about my first book, *"It's Your Turn Find Your Authentic Self and Go Fetch It"* and that my second book, *"Power in Midlife and Beyond"* is ready to be published. Looking at me intently she gave me a challenging revelation. She said, "Miss Barbara, your book is not finished." I smile when she would call me "Miss" because "miss" is a title of respect when a woman is your elder in the African American Heritage. Reverend Demett is from South Carolina. No surprise. I was startled and surprised when she said my book is not finished. You must add another chapter, she said, that talks about your love for your daughter, faith in God's Grace and Mercy, determination and courage to be by Sherri's side for three months in this hospital. You would honor Sherri's life. Telling your story could help many people learn how you relied on God's faith, strength, and discovered inner power during a time of extreme loss. While listening to Reverend Demett's words; I thought this is the last thing I want to do is to write another chapter. My book is done. This was not a time to think about my book. I was feeling overwhelmed and all I wanted to do was to support my daughter with love, and give her whatever she needed to help her transition peacefully without pain. I was on auto-pilot, focused on being by her side every day.

A few months after Sherri's beautiful home going service; I still did not think about publishing my book. Jane Fonda, once said, that God reaches us in our wounds not our successes. One day, my husband persuaded me to go to one of our favorite flea markets. I knew I needed to get out of the house and this would be good way to spend time doing what I love – perusing flea markets. I found one popular vendor selling silver jewelry. The merchant came over to me while I was looking at a silver ring. She looked at me pensively, and asked if I was a doctor. I was startled at her question because I thought she was checking to see if I needed any help. I said yes, but I'm not a medical doctor. I'm an educator. I quickly thought that maybe something was physically wrong with her. Customers were milling around her booth, intently looking at her jewelry, but she kept looking at me. She quietly said, almost whispering, she just received a call from the hospital where her son is in Florida. The doctor said she will have to think about putting her son in a hospice. She was advised to come to the hospital immediately. I didn't even think about why she was telling me this. I remember instantly whispering to her that I buried my daughter last month. She put her hand to her mouth and she said, "Oh my God, how are you still standing?" I said, only by the Grace and power of God. I held her hand and said, you will get through this. I will pray for you. She thanked me for sharing. She apologized for sharing sad information about her son. She said, I just got the call and felt like I was going to pass out. She looked up, saw my face and knew that she had to share her story with me. I knew with unwavering faith that this was a God thing or God wink. It was a moment in time when we both benefited from our shared experience.

These two experiences motivated me to add another chapter to this book. As a result of many prayers, talking to my husband, my younger daughter Monique and grief resources; I made the decision to write about my journey with Sherri.

I'm dedicating this chapter to honor my daughter Sherri and dedicate this book to her memory. Sherri taught me about strength, humility, determination and faith. Thinking about the merchant at the flea market; maybe my experience will help women discover inner power in the worse times and the best times in life.

Sherri moved to Atlanta in 2007 when the breast cancer was in remission. Her sudden decision was surprising. Sometimes I wonder, knowing how extremely independent she was, if moving to Atlanta was to distance herself from family. I remember when Sherri was four years old, her independent nature, riding her bicycle around Cheyney University's quadrangle while waiting for me to finish taking a class. She waved at students passing by her with not a care in the world. Although that was not the way I was feeling while watching her with a cautious eye out of the window.

Sherri always avoided worrying me about anything that was not going well in her life. I only heard from her when life was going well. Our distance created a rollercoaster mother-daughter relationship. Trying her best to protect me from the disease; she only wanted me to be happy and enjoy life. She was happy when I married Ben. She told him; I know my mom will be taken care of. But as a mother, there is not much that can be hidden. Mothers always know when they are needed. I worried and tried hard to support her and be by her side when she was fighting breast cancer.

While she was in Atlanta, she fought her battles with breast cancer – always putting work first. She was a project manager at Delta Airlines. She never complained when she battled the cancer with a double mastectomy and chemotherapy.

In 2013, when the breast cancer was aggressive, she continued working every day. One day I received a call that Sherri had not reported to work in three days. I was frantic making calls as we prepared to leave for Atlanta. Her manager at Delta said, "We found Sherri." Through many calls and connecting with police in Atlanta, we discovered that Sherri was in a car accident. The police said she didn't want to go to the hospital. We discovered that she didn't remember how she got to the hospital. When we arrived in Atlanta, the doctor suspected Sherri had a seizure driving home from work. My heart still pains when I think about her being alone during the terrifying ordeal.

Fast forward. My husband and I were on automatic pilot by Sherri's side as we moved to the process of helping her stay alive. The doctors informed us that the seizure was the cancer spreading to her brain. I was devastated.

Sherri and I had many conversations about what's next. I tried to meet any of her requests. I hugged her, rubbed her feet that ached from neuropathy, and enjoyed getting her favorite foods. Talking on her cellphone was difficult as the brain cancer was spreading. I dialed numbers that she needed when she was trying to manage her health as best she could. Sherri was always in control of what she needed to do until she knew she could no longer to do it alone. Close friends and co-workers visited Sherri every day. The doctors and nurses were always attentive.

As Sherri experienced her last few days in the hospital, doctors talked to Sherri with compassion, and supported her decision to let go when they could not do anymore to maintain her life with continued treatment. Finally, the doctors told Sherri that nothing more could be done that would be humane to her health. That was one of the most difficult days to watch my daughter listen to what the doctors were telling her with dignity and faith. I will never forget that day.

Monique visited the hospital to be with her sister on several occasions. Her strength and love for Sherri helped me. She traveled with her husband Eric, and my granddaughters, Mecca and Micah to visit Sherri. They loved their Auntie Sherri. Monique worked tirelessly to find the best hospice for Sherri in Atlanta. There were many obstacles in our path trying to put Sherri in a peaceful and loving place to live out the rest of her time. By God's miracle, a hospice was found for Sherri. It was beautiful with the most compassionate doctors and nurses.

Our beloved Sherri Lisa Moore was born in Atlantic City, New Jersey on September 2, 1964. She lived in West Philadelphia, PA and Sharon Hill, Pennsylvania. Sherri was an active student in Overbrook High School enjoying her love of sports playing basketball on the varsity team. Her ability to excel in academics was evident achieving high grades, especially in math.

She was active in Jimmy's Juniors Bowling Team Association, in Philadelphia. Mr. Franklin Hardwell was one of the founders of Jimmy's Juniors. He coached hundreds of children to learn how to bowl, understand sportsmanship and life skills. Sherri was not only an active bowler, but participated in the organization as an officer. She and her sister Monique competed with many bowling teams across the country.

Sherri continued her education by achieving a Doctorate of Business Administration, as a doctoral candidate, at the University of Phoenix, Masters of Business Administration, at Eastern College, PA, Bachelor of Science Degree in Business Administration, at Temple University, and Associates of Science Degree in Computer Science/MIS at Delaware Community College. Sherri was an excellent student known for her analytical and marketing skills.

Sherri was employed at Independence Blue Cross (IBC) as Senior Telecommunications Analyst, First Union (Wachovia Bank), Telecommunications Technology Officer, and Wells Fargo Home Mortgage, Mortgage Consultant.

In 2002, Sherri created her own business, Avanti Mortgage, Inc.   Sherri was excited to finally be her own boss. She loved working with clients and customers. People always trusted Sherri's knowledge of banking and business. Sherri's excellent customer service skills were evident in helping people live a better life owning their own home.

Sherri decided to move to Atlanta, Ga., because she was tired of the cold weather in Philadelphia. Her goal was to work as a flight attendant for Delta Airlines. She was thrilled and excited to receive a call to apply to Delta Airlines. The Delta training program was extremely challenging but she passed with high marks. Several years later Sherri was selected to participate on a special project to enhance customer service for Delta employees.

Sherri touched many lives with her beautiful smile, warm nurturing quality, and her fun ways. She demanded in her quiet way, for people to get along and to be nice to each other. Sherri will always be remembered for her unselfish and caring ways.

We will miss you Sherri. You have a place in our hearts. You impacted our lives in many ways. May we learn from your quiet Spirit to always keep the peace. A passage from her favorite scripture, Phil4:4-9, "Rejoice! Let your gentleness be evident to all."

I was amazed at the hospital, hospice and funeral regarding how many people's lives Sherri touched. It was overwhelming to know that my daughter and our family were truly loved by many, many people. Sherri left me knowing that she was special.

God reaches me in my most difficult moments by going deep inside my soul and lifting out the power within me to bare the grief. The power within helps me to withstand a pain that I've been told heals in time. Rationally, I know the healing cycle is a human experience that touches everyone. When Sherri left to be with God, I felt a huge void that could not be filled.

There will always be a void in my heart for Sherri. God is showing me how to press on beyond the void. This is what *"Power in Midlife and Beyond"* is about. Filling the voids created by just living – retirement, losing loved ones, beginning again, and rediscovering our authentic self.

Power in Midlife and Beyond

"The privilege of a lifetime is being who we are."

Joseph Campbell

Dealing With a Financial Crisis

Today's questionable economy is impacting how we live. Finding ways to budget expenses, pay bills, save for children's college educations, and enjoying the simple things in life, such as going to a movie and eating popcorn, are major challenges for many families.

Fear of being laid off, in the face of millions of people losing their jobs, is paramount. When the recession will change for the better no one really knows. All we know is that right now, finding ways to pay the bills is critical.

In November 2010, a study *"New Unemployables"* by Boston College's Sloan Center on Aging & Work and the Heldrich Center for Workforce Development at Rutgers University, reveals how adults 55+ are facing challenges in finding a job and may remain out of work longer than younger job seekers. The study cites that people 55 and over seem to recognize that their strengths are not effective, 64% of older job seekers rated the job search tools not helpful compared to less than half (49%) of younger job seekers. This is a significant study that links to my belief that mid-lifers require a different form of job seeking.

Job seeking during midlife or after retirement means discovering or rediscovering your authentic self. Those of us facing midlife changes are also trying to cope with making difficult financial decisions. My hope is that this book will be a resource to help you return to the past and realize – you're more than you think you are. Reading this book will help you to discover natural strengths that will create financial abundance.

I remember in elementary school I dreamed of becoming a teacher. When I graduated from college my first teaching position was fourth grade in the Philadelphia School District, in 1969. Teaching was comfortable and brought me joy. Little did I know my first year of teaching would force me to discover an unknown natural strength.

In 1969, I experienced a major school strike that lasted for almost one year. The school strike was a negative and fearful experience. I was faced with a difficult marriage on the brink of a divorce, and raising two daughters alone. I was under a lot of pressure to not cross the picket line, and I was in a bad financial situation trying to make ends meet during the strike. Many teachers were victims of phone threats or vandalism to cars and homes. I was forced to seek welfare and collect food stamps to feed my children. Not knowing when the strike would end, I tried to find alternative ways to pay my bills.

I thought hard about what I could do that comes easy to me and would not require additional training. My thoughts went as far back as high school. What did I do in high school that I enjoyed? Well, I loved watching plays and movies and would often write plays at school. Then, I asked myself how I could make money using my writing skills. While watching "Sesame Street" with my daughters, I wondered if they paid writers to write live segments for Elmo and Ernie. Remembering my strength was a huge "Aha! moment" for me. I followed my gut instinct, took a chance, and called Children's Television Workshop (CTW). I found out that CTW paid writers $25 per script for segments with Ernie and other puppets. Today it doesn't seem like a lot of money, but $25 per script would help me balance my income during the strike. So I submitted scripts for the segments, and received a check in the mail.

After teaching 10 years, I decided that my teaching income was not enough to raise two daughters and send them to college. I was fortunate to work with a career counselor to restructure my resume. My revised resume focused on my experience in working with adults in training communication skills at local non-profit organizations during the summer. My new career goal was to be a corporate human resource trainer. I was offered a position as Manager of Training and Development with a major health care provider in Philadelphia, PA. During my tenure as a corporate executive, I paid attention to skills that came easy to me.

In 1988, while working for the health care organization, I was asked to be a training consultant for the Naval Defense Department in Philadelphia, which is now a closed facility. When the department told about 10,000 people that they no longer had jobs, I was asked to create a training program to help those employees learn ways to find careers that would help them survive. Many of the employees worked at the facility for a number of years and thought they would spend their entire careers in that job. For many employees, their job at the Navy Defense Department was their first and only job. Many possessed only a GED, and the job market challenged them to find ways to make a living. Many of the employees were devastated, lost and shocked that they would have to look for a job. This contract was one of the most challenging training programs to design. I knew that it would be difficult to motivate the employees because their need to survive was not being met.

Thinking about how I could help the employees, I tried to imagine what I would do if I was faced with the same devastating situation. What would I do if I had little or no training, but had to find a new job?

I incorporated exercises to help the employees to write life stories to discover natural strengths. These life stories surfaced memories of strengths that came easy to them. Many people in the class discovered strengths as carpenters, good cooks or housekeepers, great with children. An older woman who worked at the center since she was 18 remembered that she bakes the best bread. Family and friends loved her bread. So, we helped her to create an action plan to sell bread in her neighborhood, at her church and figured out various vendor opportunities in the city. Paying her phone bill and her rent was her immediate need until she could find a job, and selling bread helped her do that.

The training program was successful because we helped people rewind to the past to discover their natural strengths that would increase their income after being terminated from their jobs. Many employees decided to return to school to learn a trade or challenge themselves to take courses at a community college. During the training class we asked people to dialogue with a partner and discuss a learning experience in high school that brought them joy. Several of the employees recalled favorite subjects in high school – history, writing or a trade. These discussions helped employees to remember that they are not leaving their jobs without any skills. The discussions gave the employees a sense of accomplishment they could build on in the training.

Many people today are experiencing financial challenges due to the loss of retirement money or not knowing how to find a job after being laid off. Discovering natural strengths is one way to survive while looking for employment. This book will help you find your strengths to lessen the impact of these difficult times in our national economy.

Creating the life you deserve — knowing you are more than you think you are — by using your natural strengths to do the things you love, brings you joy and gives you a peaceful feeling that you are in your "dharma," knowing your purpose in life. It is a wonderful feeling when you are in the zone of life, saying "So this is what it feels like to be truly me." This is what I call "authentic living." You will discover various techniques in this book to discover or rediscover your authentic self. When you are living authentically, you will find the resources you need to create financial abundance.

I love this quote by Dr. Phil McGraw, also known as "Dr. Phil," which describes living an authentic life: "The authentic self is the you that can be found at your absolute core. It is the part of you not defined by your job, function, or role. It is the composite of all your skills, talents and wisdom. It is all of the things that are uniquely yours and need expression, rather than what you believe you are supposed to be and do."

This book outlines my 14 "Funthentic" tips to help you surface your natural gifts. I purposely offer tips that would not take too much time. What it will take is determination, curiosity, and a willingness to try the tips and see what happens.

Experiencing all the "Aha! moments," or what I call "Silver Star Clues," that will surface when you discover/rediscover hidden talents and skills, will be fun.

Part I

"You cannot be anything you want to be, but you can be a lot more of who you already are." **Best-selling author Tom Rath, in "StrengthsFinder 2.0"**

Chapter 1 – Discovering Natural Strengths in Midlife Transformation

People often ask me how to plan for the next phase in life when retiring is not an option. Current life expectancy for Americans is 80; therefore people born in 1946 could possibly live an added 30 years. All those millions of boomers are probably trying to figure out how they will continue to lead a productive life for at least a few more decades.

In *"The Existential Necessity of Midlife Change,"* published in Harvard Business Review (February 2008), Carlo Strenger states that changes in midlife are a critical workforce issue. Many folks are ill-prepared for changes in midlife, and it can help to look at the myths related to midlife transition.

"The perception that mid-life is the onset of decline", Strenger says, "is based on historically outdated conceptions. The notion that mid-life is a magical transformation is yet another myth." Vision and willpower can't do it all.

Following decades of research with entrepreneurs and executives age 50 and older, Strenger believes these myths inhibit a successful midlife career change. His belief is that dreams must be connected to our potential; otherwise, they are idle fantasies. People can rid themselves of wishful thinking by concentrating on the connection between their skills and aspirations.

Organizations need to take radical steps to help their executives understand that everybody in the company will leave it at some point and begin another life.

With my clients, I support that notion, and I also promote the idea of self-discovery. Finding your authentic self is the work that makes second career dreams become reality.

People who experience the impact of midlife transformation during early retirement or retirement find it challenging. Trying to figure out at that point what you should do with your life, can be troubling. Many retirees dreamed of spending the retirement traveling, giving back to the community, and just enjoying life without financial burdens. Retirement savings were supposed to take care of the "golden years." If working during midlife is a necessity, then working authentically can be a golden opportunity. Why not do something that feels natural — something that demonstrates strengths that are characteristics of your true self?

"Reappraise the past, reevaluate where we've been, clarify where we are, and predict or anticipate where we are headed." American author, social activist and college professor Toni Cade Bambara

Living authentically — living a truthful life — feels correct. You move with the ease and flow of the universe. As the world sends you challenges, your authentic self knows how to respond. Using fun and exciting tips to help discover/rediscover your authentic self leads you to a world of "knowing." Knowing who you are feels like a beaming, bright light of self-awareness. The bright light is symbolic of silver. I love to wear silver jewelry. During my midlife transformation I was drawn to silver. Silver represents living a bright and beaming light that glows, thus finding my "Silver Star Clues."

In her book, *"The Age of Miracles: Embracing the New Mid-life,"* Marianne Williamson says, "How you'll inhabit the space of mid-life and beyond is an open question that only you can answer. If you choose the path of least resistance – nonresistance not in a Taoist way but in a lazy way – then gravity will overwhelm you. You'll grow old with little grace or joy. But if you claim for yourself another possibility, you'll open the door to something decidedly new."

I want to support men and women in discovering new possibilities for their second phase of life. The second phase of our journey is impacted by hormonal changes, feeling a void, and not knowing what is missing – we just know something in our life has changed. We are no longer patient with situations that at one time were easier to manage. Recognition of mortality is present in the second phase of life – the recognition that all of a sudden life feels like "Wow, there isn't much time to do what I wanted to do." Even though we are living longer, age is irrelevant. What I feel like at 50 predicts what I will feel like when I am 80 or 90. Rediscovering who you are can help the aging years feel more like your true self.

Deciding on what to do next may feel overwhelming – coping with health issues, empty nest syndrome, the poor economy and wondering when is a good time to retire? – or can I even retire? – take up a lot of thinking when trying to understand the feelings of this second phase of our life.

The second phase of life is a wake-up call to move towards our whole self. I remember how midlife was challenging for me – I was filled with anxiety of what to do next with my life while coping with everyday living. I wrote this book to help women embrace midlife and move forward knowing that the second phase of our lives can be exciting.

In her book *"The Female Brain,"* Dr. Louann Brizendine shares how women's brains and hormones impact decisions in different stages of their lives, such as career decisions and with whom we fall in love. She says, "At menopause, the female brain is nowhere near ready to retire. As a matter of fact, many women's lives are just hitting their peak. This can be an exciting intellectual time now that the burden of rearing children has decreased and the preoccupation of the mommy brain is lessened. The contribution of work to a woman's personality, identity, and fulfillment once again becomes as important as it may have been before the mommy brain took over." Dr. Brizendine adds that work and accomplishment can be critical to a woman's sense of well-being during this life transition. "There is a lot of life after menopause, and embracing work – whatever that may be – passionately, clearly, allows a woman to feel regenerated and fulfilled," she states.

First of all, let's be honest. The challenges of midlife can become a force that shakes our inner core to begin the search for something that maybe we forgot and we need to go find, quickly. Many of us have moments in midlife that feel like a void or a sense of not being on the same page with others. It is difficult to explain because getting through midlife is not a simple process. However, mid-life can be the most wonderful opportunity to discover/rediscover who you really are. What slate of talents and skills did you bring into this world? Beginning now to grow into your natural state of authenticity is critical. You have to let go of situations, experiences, and things that we let define who we are and become who you really are in life. Yes, for some, midlife can be painful. Avoiding the pain in midlife is a prognosis for a meaningless life. Not knowing who you are leaves you vulnerable to be swept by the winds of someone else's definition of who you are.

In her book *"Awakening at Mid-life,"* Dr. Kathleen Brehony describes how the failure to experience the true psychological transformation of the midlife passage can leave us stuck in a half-crazy place. You are not by yourself in this midlife experience – Brehony says 81 million people today struggle with the powerful changes of midlife experiences. In her book she explains the process of self-fulfilling one's destiny by following one's unique path of development. It is not just a personality theory development by 20th century psychologists, such as Maslow, Jung, Carl Rogers, Fritz Perls, and Alfred Adler, "but an idea that has resonated in all cultures throughout the history of the human race," she states. She adds that the Navajo call the midlife journey "the Pollen Path," the Sioux named it "The Good Red Road," Chinese simply say "Tao." I think we are the only country that calls midlife transformation a "crisis."

Living authentically is a call to do your "inner work." Dr. Brehony says, "We live in a culture that does not honor inner work, instead, it insists on defining goals and moving swiftly toward them. We are often told, or we tell ourselves to just make a decision and stick to it, or we ask ourselves, 'When are you going to get over this?'" Inner work toward finding the true self is like going on an archeological dig, as Sarah Ban Breathnach describes in her book, "Simple Abundance," the journey begins with you. This is an opportune time to allow yourself to grow from within – corporations need you to go within to compete in the marketplace. It is not for the sake of just achieving creativity – the call from corporate America – but a wonderful time to feel free to give yourself permission to go within and rediscover or discover the true sense of who you are.

There are many benefits in beginning the journey to discover hidden strengths and skills.

- You deserve to create the career and life you want.

- You deserve to know the truth about who you are and believe that it is all good.

- You are more than you think you are.

- You are worth doing the work to gain authentic power.

- Rediscover the person you forgot due to life's demands and detours.

You can discover your authentic self while working in an organization – you can also demonstrate your authentic self while working. Be careful. Life kicks in and impacts our direction/decisions/personality. Time robs us of taking a look at ourselves – Well, guess what? IT'S YOUR TURN NOW!!!

"Always be the first-rate version of yourself,
instead of a second-rate version of somebody else."
Singer and actress, Judy Garland

Chapter 2 – Living Authentically Surfaces Your Natural Strengths

Authentic living is when you embrace all of the wonderful things you know are true about who you are and let them shine. You don't have to talk about it, you are being who you are, and you are confident. Authentic living is when you have the courage to say "no" to people or events that don't work for you or have your best interest in mind.

Poet and author Grace Paley believes an authentic life is "a life that's truthful.

You're alive – you don't do work you hate – you do the things you believe in. That's authentic."

Your natural strength comes through with little or no effort, and with a look of joy or contentment.

Watch children and you will see what being authentic looks like. I love watching my granddaughter work out a puzzle. I gave Mecca her first puzzle when she was 3 years old. It was exciting to see how easily she was able to fit the pieces together. While she tries to figure out where each piece fits she verbalizes why it makes sense to begin with certain colors. Mecca was not taught how to work with puzzles. I would say she was born with this natural ability.

The natural talents of a friend's daughter became obvious to me when the girl was only 2 years old. As her mother and I talked, and she sat in a nearby high chair, she spoke in well-versed sentences not typical for a girl her age. It was obvious there was something special about this child. Her mother was a gifted singer and her father was a famous R&B songwriter. Almost 22 years later I watched that young girl sing in a musical theatre production. She was beautiful and her voice was amazing. As the saying goes, "The apple does not fall far from the tree." That girl was fortunate to have parents that recognized her talents and nurtured her gift at an early age.

Recognizing talents at an early age gives children a jumpstart in knowing who they are. Many children are not this fortunate – some have a gift that goes unrecognized for years or maybe is never recognized at all.

Tom Rath, author of *StrengthsFinder 2.0*, describes a New Zealand longitudinal study of 1,000 children over a 23-year period, which revealed that a child's observed personality at age 3 shows remarkable similarity to his or her reported personality traits at age 26. This is why, Rath explains, *StrengthsFinder* measures the elements of your personality that are less likely to change – your talents.

As psychiatrist Carl Jung implies, we did not come into this world with a blank slate – we came into this world to seek wholeness. We inherited our DNA and physical characteristics from our parents and ancestors, and we inherited emotional qualities that play out in our behavior. Most importantly, we inherited talents and strengths that we don't even know exist because these gems are hidden or forgotten as life kicks in. Or we become distracted from who we really are while we move on a path of survival or what we were told to pursue.

In Henry Louis Gates Jr.'s documentary *"African American Lives,"* Gates reveals interesting facts about prominent African Americans' ancestors. Gates' revelations helped celebrities such as comedian Chris Rock, reflect on talents and life choices.

Knowing the talents and skills of your family members or ancestors provide valuable clues to what you can do that comes with the least amount of effort. This information puts you a step further to finding your true self.

Living authentically is letting your true voice be heard.

"I'd tell myself to listen to my heart. Listen to that little voice that says, 'Mmm, I don't think so.' Because, when you override that, you basically override who you are." **Actress, Glenn Close**

Chapter 3 – Women: Speaking Your Truth

When a woman is living authentically, she allows her voice to be heard. Many times women let our voices get drowned out by men. The workplace creates unspoken norms that silence us and when we want to speak our truth we are afraid of losing our jobs. Some people make us feel invisible because they assume what we have to say or think is not important. Speaking your truth means saying what you mean from the deepest part of yourself.

Some women find it difficult to speak their truth when someone verbally attacks them or makes them feel badly. Don't bury it! You authentically speak your truth. Now there is a way to say it! No twisting heads, hands on your hips, or pointing or raising your voice. When you are being authentic, you are as calm as you can be, but your voice is strong.

My journey to speaking my truth in conversations with men has been one of the most challenging parts of seeking my authentic self. Six years into my second marriage, to a wonderful man, I found conversations with him challenging and frustrating at times. I realized we had different ways of communicating. This was not new, but it became increasingly difficult to dialogue about even mundane topics. When I asked too many questions, I was met with annoyance or, "Why do you need to know a lot of information?"

One day, after my husband returned from a massage, I asked him if the masseuse was a younger or older woman. I believed this was a question that most women would ask, out of curiosity, not insecurity. My husband did not take this question in the same light.

Depending on the topic, his response to my questions usually ended with shutting me down and suppressing my voice. This felt awful because I felt like I was suffocating. The words were left stuck in my throat with nowhere to go.

My "Aha! moment" came after reading a book by Dr. Aaron T. Beck, director of the Center for Cognitive Therapy at the University of Pennsylvania. In the book *"Love is Never Enough,"* he explains the difference in conversational styles between men and women. He describes how questioning is a normal way to carry on a conversation. However, questioning can lead to misunderstanding and distress between men and women. I thought questioning was a way to engage in a conversation. Dr. Beck says women tend to show a greater tendency to ask questions. Most researchers believe that women's propensity for question-asking indicates their investment in maintaining routine interactions between people. Beck goes on to add men are less likely than women to ask personal questions. Men are prone to think, "If she wants to tell me something, she'll tell me without my asking." A woman might reflect, "If I don't ask, he'll think that I don't care." For men, questions may represent intrusive meddling and an invasion of privacy; for women, they are a sign of intimacy and an expression of caring. My husband was a 30-year State Police veteran. He has an authoritative voice and his tendency to react to questions negatively paired with his tone of voice created stress in our conversations.

Dr. Beck's observations were helpful in understanding what was creating a barrier to speaking my truth. Now, the work is the practice and I realize that differences are good, not bad – they need to be recognized and valued. I am happy to say my ability to communicate with my husband, and with other men, has improved.

Gary Zukav, author of *"The Seat of the Soul"* says, "An authentically empowered person is someone who is humble – not false humility, one who stoops to be with someone they perceive to be lower than him or her. It is an inclusiveness of one who responds to the beauty of each soul."

Being authentic is when you embrace all the wonderful things you know are true about who you are and let them shine – you don't have to talk about it; you are being who you are. People will notice the difference because you are confident.

When you have the courage to say "no" to people and events that don't work for you —and mean it! — and not be afraid that you will fall off the face of the earth or the person you said "no" to will fall apart, that's being authentic.

Saying "no" is a gift to our souls. Saying "no" sends out a message that "this is who I am, I deserve to say 'no' to what is not working for me. I have the right to say 'no' to people who create negative energy for me." Yes, I know it is not always easy and can be one of the challenging lessons in life.

I practiced saying "no" in the beginning of my transformation. I was, of course, nervous. I felt a sense of trepidation saying "no" because it was different for me. I grew up trying to please people in order to affirm and validate me. This continued into my early adult years. Finally, I got the message when a doctor told me "you bounced your checkbook. You took too much of yourself out and gave it away to everyone, and did not replace it with you to balance out your life." Living authentically empowers you to make effective decisions that are aligned with your core values. Do you know what you believe is true for yourself? Do you know your absolute bottom line in dealing with a difficult person? Do you know what you believe spiritually? You and only you are responsible to create the authentic life you deserve.

I like this quote by Eleanor Roosevelt, one of my favorite women leaders.

"One's philosophy is not best expressed in words; it is expressed in the choices one makes. In the long run, we shape our lives and we shape ourselves. The process never ends until we die. And, the choices we make are ultimately our own responsibility."

Being authentic means you did your inner work, which communicates to the world that you are someone who is responsible for yourself and that you want everyone to know this is who you are.

"Let us be among those who believe that the inner transformation of our lives is a goal worth of our best effort." **Richard Foster**

Chapter 4 – Knowing Your Authentic Self Prepares You for a Dynamic Second Career

I am the product of a strong West Indian culture in which education was paramount. Attending college was not a choice, it was a decision made by my parents. Following the career path of a teacher was based on economic survival. Fortunately, teaching was a path I wanted to follow, so my mother made sure I worked as a summer camp counselor at "Star Lake," a wonderful Salvation Army camp. That was where I developed my love for working with children. I appreciate the guidance I received from my parents and grandparents. They prepared me for a life to feel free to make effective, authentic career choices.

It was not until I was in my 30s that I realized there was more to me than being a teacher. I love teaching and I still teach at a university – as I discussed in my first book *It's Your Turn: Find Your Authentic Self and Go Fetch It!* – the midlife nudge that I experienced clearly pushed me to find more of my natural talents and gifts.

Two years ago, Monique, my youngest daughter, gave me a book signing at her home. I was thrilled at her offer to invite her friends to hear me speak because her gesture affirmed that she supported and believed in me. Most of her invited guests would be between the ages of 25 and 45. I began to question whether her friends would relate to my talk about rediscovering/discovering their natural talents and skills since my audience tends to be women who are facing retirement or retired. Monique said, "Mom, my friends want to hear how you created three authentic careers." They want to begin planning now for second careers while they are working. "Many of my friends," she said, are working in careers that are not congruent with who they are. She convinced me that my words would be relevant to their needs.

As Monique's friends arrived to the book signing I noticed how excited they were about gathering with almost 40 women to talk about living authentic lives. I didn't realize Monique knew that many beautiful and successful women. Many of the women had one or two children between the ages of 10 months and 5 years old. I looked around the room and wondered if I could convince these women to take time out of their busy lives to discover their authentic selves. Most of these women had corporate positions while raising small children. I asked these women what they wanted me to share with them. They all had a sense of urgency to start now and not wait until they are nearing retirement to find out who they really are. They needed to begin the process of defining their true selves in order to prepare for an authentic second career before they feel the effects of midlife – before thoughts of retirement begins to feel like reality. It appeared that many women in the room were working at jobs out of necessity, not out of joy. They weren't necessarily doing what came easy to them.

I realized it was important to not make our discussion feel like additional work for the women. Most of them complained they already didn't have enough time and were stressed. How could they fit in time to go on an "archaeological dig," as I did, was the main topic of our discussion. One woman remarked that it takes time to do inner work – and though she knew it was important to do now, discovering her true self felt like a luxury. Many of the women were working in careers that were not fulfilling yet they needed to pay bills and raise a family. The economic times were challenging these women to do what they have to do work – whether it was something they enjoyed was a luxury to think about. My challenge was to convince them that there are ways to begin thinking about who they really are in the midst of challenging parental and/or professional working roles.

The discussion continued with, "How do we take off our 'supermom/superwoman hats' and begin saying 'It's my turn now,'" in the midst of taking care of their families and working?

I had my work cut out for me. I could feel a sense of urgency in the room. I shared how important it is to say "no" to things that were barriers to fulfilling their dreams and goals. Their eyes were saying to me, "Are you kidding?" Saying "no" is not a choice when raising children and working at jobs that demand long hours. Well, no, I was not kidding. Saying "no" is an option we all have. True, parenting and working long hours does not provide many opportunities to say "no" often, however finding ways to lessen the burden of feeling you cannot say "no" is the main concern. Readiness to finding your authentic self is creating space to begin the discovery process.

Busy mothers who work eight hours or more each day have lots of demands on their time. They may or may not be able to take lunch breaks. They pick up children after school, fix dinner and organize play dates. Somewhere between all of this activity is a chunk of time – maybe 15 to 20 minutes out of the day to think about you. While driving the car, find some space for yourself between thinking about tasks for your children and family. If exercise is mandatory, then think about you while walking the treadmill. This is your time of day to do your inner work.

My discovery journey began while raising my children as a single parent. Watching my daughter graduate from Freedom Theatre, I heard a poem titled *"Who Am I?"* This was the beginning of my transformation. How did I find the time to be truthful? I told the group of women about how I began to read books to help me to help me understand what I was searching for inside of me. I decided to see a therapist to remove the fear of looking inward. I attended personal growth seminars in between working, taking care of my children, and attending classes to receive my master's degree and doctorate. You see, I was extremely determined to find my true self. I would not allow other people to decide what I should do and should not do with my life anymore. Most importantly, I created a vision for how I wanted to live my life when my daughters were no longer financially dependent on me.

Yes, I told the women, there is a light at the end of the tunnel. Suddenly, you turn around and no one needs you anymore – and then you ask, "What do I do now?" I did not want that to happen to me. My grandmother always told me that education is power and it helps you make your own choices in life. The women started to listen intently now because they could relate with the comments. My grandmother's guidance was the impetus for me to work hard continuing my education because I knew I would have to make career choices that suited me and were congruent to my authentic self.

I spoke to a group of parents who are part of Jack and Jill of America, Inc., an African American organization of mothers "who nurture future leaders by strengthening children ages 2-19 through chapter programming, community service, legislative advocacy, and philanthropic giving." After my presentation, a woman came up to me and thanked me for giving her a major "Aha! moment." She said, she realized that even though she valued being an anesthesiologist, she realized how much she loves to cook and always valued her skill in cooking. She decided she would pursue her dream of being a chef while raising her children. She figured by the time they were in high school she would be able to begin taking a few courses. Her dream may not begin immediately – but planning now was an investment in doing her inner work to prepare her for her midlife transformation. She was rediscovering her true self.

"Every decision you make – every decision – is not a decision about what to do. It's a decision about Who You Are. When you see this, when you understand it, everything changes. You begin to see life in a new say. All events, occurrences, and situations turn into opportunities to do what you came here to do." **Neale Donald Walsch, Author** *"Conversations With God"*

Chapter 5 – What Does Living Authentically Feel Like?

In his article, *"Defining Your Authentic Self,"* posted on his website, Dr. Phil McGraw describes the opposite of authentic self as the "fictional self."

"When you're not living faithfully to your authentic self, you find yourself feeling incomplete, as if there is a hole in your soul. You may have found that it's easier to fill the roles your family and friends expect of you, rather than becoming who you really want to be. Living this way drains you of the critical life energy you need to pursue the things you truly value." When you live a life that has you ignoring your true gifts and talents while performing assigned or inherited roles instead, Dr. Phil says, you are living as your fictional self. I love these statements because Dr. Phil's words are aligned with my belief about the importance of living an authentic life.

A dear friend of mine – the Rev. Susan Teegan-Case, director of Arts and Spirituality Center, in Philadelphia, Pa, joined me for lunch one day. I asked her what it feels like to live a life of truth – knowing who you are. Susan said living her life of truth feels like she is in her "zone." It's a feeling of being alive, knowing that her purpose is real – she feels connected to life.

Feeling authentic is a sense of satisfaction in knowing who you are. You carry yourself with an air of self-acceptance. For me, it feels like the grace of God is allowing me to live with an inner peace – knowing that I am not an accident in life, that there is purpose for me being here and I am enjoying this ride of finding out what it is.

Authentic living is consistently being open to the question of "who am I?" It is saying to yourself: "I am open to discover, I am open to rediscover, I am open to live authentically," and trusting the universe to send you what you need to know about who you are. My daily experiences connect me to being fully conscious of the connection and what the connection says about who I am.

An experience in a hospital cafeteria reinforced my belief that when you communicate your authentic self, you are in sync with the universe and good things come your way.

While waiting for my husband to finish a doctor's appointment I went in the cafeteria to eat my breakfast. I waited in line to pay for my food and when I handed the cashier my credit card, she apologized and said the cafeteria did not accept credit cards. I had a substantial amount of food on my plate, but resigned myself to the fact that I'd have to leave it there and go to the ATM. I proceeded to move my tray when suddenly a lady standing next to me said, "Don't worry," as she paid for my food. I was surprised and grateful that this stranger would pay for my breakfast. I kept saying thank you, but she held up her hand and quickly left, disappearing into the crowded cafeteria. I understood her wish to leave and avoid effusive comments – I think she was saying, "It's OK, my blessings will come back in return." I thought about her act of kindness for a long time. I felt blessed – I also believe that what we give out we get back.

In a *Psychology Today* magazine article titled
"Dare to be Yourself" (June 2008) by Karen Wright,
described the opposite of being authentic as "inauthentic."
Though no such word exists in the dictionary, the author
described inauthentic as a "vague feeling of
dissatisfaction," or feeling dissatisfied with yourself and
not being able to put the feelings into words. Maybe the
thoughts were, "You know this is not you." Then what is it
that I should be doing that is really me? Or when you keep
hearing a voice or feel a nudge on your shoulder or a
whisper in your ear saying to you, "Now you know this is
not you" or "Who are you trying to fool," or a strong
feeling of "I don't like doing this anymore." You feel like
a square peg in a round hole.

People often ask me, "When am I going to know
what I am supposed to do with my life?" When I asked the
same question the universe sent me answers. I trusted God
and trusted the process of self-discovery knowing that there
was a light at the end of my dark tunnel of not knowing
who I am. I focused on the question – watched and waited
for clues, sometimes a hint or an experience surfaced
answers to "what." I left myself open and let the universe
"do its thing." Actually, the "when" is happening now.

For me, the question of who I am has
metamorphosed. The only way I can know what I should be
doing is if I focus on who I should be. That doesn't mean
there aren't magnificent things I am supposed to do, but
God can only work for us to the extent that He can work
through us.

We are not blank slates – we were prepared for the
experience of human life. Like the birds were ready to
build nests, or female sea turtles set to return to the site of
their hatching to lay their eggs, human beings were born
with a "blueprint" for life.

"The glass ceiling doesn't apply when you build your own house." Heidi Roizen – taken from Bits and Pieces - heresathought@ragan.com

Chapter 6 – Working Authentically

When I was a manager for training and development in a large health care organization, I attended an organizational development conference in Philadelphia. I selected to attend a "Creativity in the Workplace" seminar. This seminar was a turning point in self-discovery. The seminar leader explained that its purpose was to assess our creativity and how it impacts how we work and perceive the corporate world. Scores ranged from 0 to 149, 0 being a score that was the most extreme in perceiving the corporate environment as highly structured with the least amount of fluidity in movement – compartmentalized silos demonstrating how people would not be able to cross lines to other departments for communication. The highest score, 149, was interpreted as the most fluid organization, with no hierarchy – people were able to move up and down the organization and individual thought was rewarded.

My score was 145, and I was not surprised. I felt that someone finally understood what it felt like for me to work in a structured environment – I was like a square peg in a round hole. The seminar leader broke us up into groups according to our scores. We were instructed to draw how we see organizations. When my group completed our drawing we looked around the room and realized our picture was the complete opposite of the drawings that were in the lowest scores. We had lines crossing each other all over the page. The seminar leader explained to our group how we must feel working in an organization. Even though we were all successful in our roles – we agreed that people in our organizations tend to look at us as either mavericks or people that question the status quo – that was me, alright. I felt heard and understood and this seminar affirmed what I had been feeling for a long time. More importantly – this was a strong clue about who I really am. There is a strong part of who I am that is creative. I never realized this before that seminar. This was the beginning of my transformation to finding out my natural talents.

"Working authentically" has been a topic for the past 20 years in corporate America, but it was an anomaly. Corporate America does not support employees being authentic – following corporate norms was the goal. Fear surfaced from leaders because the perception was if employees demonstrated their true selves – who they really are – it meant chaos would exist in the organizations. Employees being themselves were seen as being out of control. Norms on how employees should behave within organizations was important to leaders, giving a sense of control. Organizational core values were guidelines for how employees should act – the gatekeepers for organizational behavior.

The word "authentic" was not articulated in organizations during the 1980s and 1990s. The focus was mainly team building, total quality management and global management. In the last five years, CEOs introduced the concept of working and leading authentically as a way to enhance productivity in the workplace. In addition, a new trend in psychology is surfacing in the workplace — Emotional Intelligence (EI) and Social Intelligence (SI), supported by books written by Daniel Goleman. Leaders are seeking to expand the understanding of how to manage emotions in the workplace – self-awareness, self-management and the ability to manage relationships are seen as important. Both of these new trends provide an opportunity for employees to work on their inner self – exhibit natural strengths and skills in a corporate culture that says "I see you."

Working authentically is demonstrating your passion, interests, and goals. Showing up authentically in the workplace is communicating the soul of who you are – opposite to feeling like you are a square peg in a round hole. I was not prepared for one of the most challenging work experiences that forced me to communicate the soul of "who I am."

I was completing my 11th year as a training manager in a company located in Philadelphia. The last four years were very challenging for me. I was successful as a manager and my performance was top rate. Then, suddenly, I was working in a hostile environment and I had reached the end of my rope physically and emotionally. During this difficult time I discovered the inner core of who I am. The last four years my director was exhibiting strange behavior with outbursts of anger and paranoia. The two women we hired were not supportive and contributed to the hostility. When I looked around at my environment – I had enough, it was time to make a decision.

In 1992, I was sitting in a manager's meeting. My thoughts were, "If you don't leave, you will not survive in this organization." These words resonated loudly. I knew this was God nudging me to do something, now! It took this situation to push me to make a decision about my future. I decided to talk to an attorney, and I'll never forget her. The universe sent me someone who immediately understood what I was dealing with – she took notes and for six months she guided me how to gather data to prepare for an exit or file a lawsuit. She was clear that the final decision on which way to go was mine. I knew in my heart that through prayer and meditation the right time to make a decision would happen and be revealed to me. I waited patiently – and one day as I attended a managers meeting, I looked around the room and felt like I was experiencing an out-of-body experience. Now I know what people mean when they say something feels surreal. In the meeting, looking around the room, I could not hear voices – I saw only moving heads and words. I heard a loud voice in my ear – I interpreted this voice as God saying loud and clear, "You must leave this meeting now and leave the company." I said to the group, "This meeting has ended for me." All the managers were shocked. I left the meeting and called my attorney and told her it was time to start the process. "I'm ready to go," I said. I saw faces with shocked expressions. All I wanted was divine justice. Six months later I received a call from the CEO – I was shocked. He apologized for how I had to leave the company. He told me that the director was fired six months later due to an investigation of his behavior.

On my journey to discover me I discovered my top core value is "integrity." This is who I am. My authentic self was challenged that day – My dilemma was will I be true to who I am and risk not knowing the outcome, and trust that God and the universe would take care of me, or remain in this hostile environment? I decided to meet my challenge head on – and demonstrate my core value – integrity. To this day, one of my top core values still remains "integrity." I wrote in my first book that sometimes connections and experiences help you to discover more about who you are. Watch what you ask for – I wanted to discover my true self. Here was a painful experience that helped me grow stronger – and the benefit was it gave me another "silver star" clue about who I am deep inside.

The end of the story is that I left the organization on my terms – I did not burn any bridges. I maintained immense support from employees and managers. I moved on to complete my doctorate, begin my business Positive Trends, Inc., and was asked to work for a large financial institution in organizational development with permission to continue my consulting business at the same time. I turned a negative situation into a positive one in my career journey.

"Never believe that a few caring people can't change the world. For, indeed that's all who ever have."
Margaret Mead, Anthropologist

Chapter 7 – Leading Authentically

Since the horrific events of Sept. 11, 2001, employees have begun to evaluate meaning in their work and question their purpose in life. Conference rooms became the focal point for combining discussions on projects with conversations on what is the point of doing them? Many people feel vulnerable and no longer take life for granted since that horrible day.

An article published in the *Harvard Business Review*, February 2007, titled *"Discovering Your Authentic Leadership,"* was based on Bill George's book, *"Authentic Leadership: Rediscovering the Secrets in Creating Lasting Value."* In it he challenged the next generation to lead authentically by demonstrating a passion for their purpose, practicing their values consistently, and leading with their hearts as well as their heads. The article reviewed a study conducted with 125 leaders, which revealed that discovering your authentic leadership requires a commitment to develop yourself.

After reading this article I questioned how managers and supervisors could motivate employees to develop their authentic selves in the company. Many people help make organizations function and be productive every day – leaders get recognized for setting the tone, vision, and mission for the organization. But how can average "workers" in lower-level positions feel authentic? And how would being authentic help people want to come to work and be creative? Why is it important for people in the workplace today to show up authentically? How can knowing who you are contribute a sense of purpose in the workplace?

Aside from bringing your learned skills to the workplace, when you bring your authentic self, your work becomes more meaningful. Being authentic at work means you are demonstrating your core values and natural strengths and talents.

Today's organizations value authentic behavior because difficult decisions challenge many employees to do the "right thing" for themselves and the organization. Working authentically exhibits a consistency in behavior that helps organizations see you more as a person to be trusted. No one has to guess who you are, your values are clear when making critical decisions or working with customers.

The article by Bill George, et.al in the *Harvard Business Review* February 2007 discussed how leaders who were surveyed contributed their success to their life stories. Many leaders stated that their life experiences helped them to discover their core values and they were able to lead organizations with a sense of purpose.

Working authentically is allowing your inner spirit to guide your feeling of being your true self in an organization. Patricia Aburdene, author of "*MegaTrends 2010: The Rise of Conscious Capitalism,*" says in an article in "*Workplace Spirituality,*" June 8, 2010, " the search for morals and meaning at work, as well as the desire to experience the peace and purpose of the Sacred in the stressful world of business, are 'inner' truths, alive in the hearts of millions of people. These internal realities profoundly influence people's behavior.....these inner truths are our values and they play a crucial role in change." She goes on to say, "As individuals, too, we live in a time of great uncertainty – the constant threat of terrorism two recent wars, unemployment, fractured IRA's and lost savings. When we find little security outside ourselves, we are forced to look within to search the heart and should for fresh answers and new directions." Aburdene believes the power of spirituality is the greatest megatrend in our era.

Sometimes your body will communicate to you whether joining a specific team was a good or bad decision, for example through restlessness, tension headaches, and feelings of guilt – the inner voice that says, "This is not you." Knowing your core values works the same way when working for an organization. When you discover your core values the career journey in an organization becomes clearer and more focused. Your core values are clearly communicated via meetings, project teams and managing employees or how you communicate to customers.

Receiving highly scored performance reviews is wonderful – but working authentically provides a satisfaction of knowing who you are, what you stand for and feeling comfortable about who you are. When all of these characteristics are aligned with the company's vision and mission you are seen as someone who is valuable to the organization. Once you discover who you are the challenge is to find an organization that supports your natural strengths and is the right fit for you.

No one can truly define who you are – managers attempt to describe your job performance in performance reviews. Unfortunately, many times an employee leaves the performance review wondering and feeling perplexed on the perceptions of the work that was communicated in the meeting. Comments in performance reviews in general are incongruent with the employee's authentic skills. Self-awareness is critically important to accurate performance reviews.

As a Human Resources consultant working in a financial services company, I experienced a challenging initiative to work with a team to lay off 40 percent of the workforce. I remember sitting in a large conference room with papers pasted on the walls of the room. On each page was the name of an employee with bullet points that listed his or her major job responsibilities. The task at hand was to review each name and offer observations about what the employee contributed to the company. The outcome was to decide who to keep in the organization and who to let go. Questions about job responsibilities were not posed as "Who is she" or "Who is he?" It was more "What have they contributed to the bottom line results of the organization?" If responses were vague, then it was evident that the employee was expendable. If the responses were more specific, demonstrating that the employee was committed and valued the goals of the organization, then he or she was generally kept. The attributes, not skills, that were communicated included:

- Motivated
- Committed
- Thinks on her feet

These attributes are not typically listed on a résumé, though you might find them listed in job summaries. More importantly, until these attributes are demonstrated in the organization, no one knows that they exist in a specific person.

Denise's Story

Denise was a participant in one of my seminars. She mentioned that she was being interviewed at her place of employment for a promotion to Director of Human Resources. She asked me if I could help her enhance her interview process using the techniques she learned in my seminar. Creating a career portfolio is one of the ways to demonstrate your authentic self in the workplace. A career portfolio is a file of work acknowledgements and positive feedback about leading specific work projects. Denise completed several activities on how to discover your authentic self. One activity was to ask a close associate at work to share with her observations about talents and skills she demonstrates with ease and little effort – that always communicate excellent results. This activity helped Denise to begin gathering a list of talents that are hidden in résumés. Authentic gifts are not necessarily the most obvious on paper. Learning about these gifts helped Denise understand so much more about herself.

I recently contacted Denise to follow up on her progress of her career. Denise got the position as Director of Human Resources where she was employed after presenting her career portfolio in the interview. Since that the time the career portfolio continues to assist Denise in developing her career. Denise updates her career portfolio to assess her accomplishments and identify her strengths. Currently, Denise is teaching on the college level, consulting in performance management and completing her Ph.D. She mentioned that she discusses with her students the importance of creating a career portfolio. Denise emphasized how important it is to know who you are when trying to create a career you deserve. Denise thanked me for introducing the "career portfolio" concept.

Working authentically in a company demonstrates that you want to be visible in the company and you stand out beyond your job responsibilities. We bring our stories to the workplace, which communicate who we are and what we have done in our lives.

An employee who motivates her team did not all of a sudden show up and demonstrate her ability to motivate people. Her story may communicate that in high school she was a team captain on a debate team or sports team. She was exposed to experiences in high school that provided an opportunity to demonstrate an authentic talent of motivating people. Asking her where or how she learned to motivate people – her response may be that she had a family role model or it came easily and naturally to her. Authenticity is being genuine and doing something that is truly who you are – a significant clue to being authentic is it comes easy to you and naturally. You do not have to be taught how to do something. It is who you are.

Finding our hidden talents and gifts in our midlife transformation may seem like a daunting experience, but it can be a fun opportunity to engage people you know in your "rediscovering who you are" journey.

People often ask me for specific examples on how to find your authentic self. I created 14 "Funthentic" tips that are fun, exciting and adventurous to help you begin your journey in rediscovering your authentic self.

1.   Talk to close friends.

2.   If you don't have a group, talk to a friend.

3.   Identify your core values.

4.   Get out of your comfort zone.

5.   Write your life story.

6.   Get help – seek therapy if needed.

7.   Brainstorm – what would you do if you were not afraid?

8.   Listen to people that say to you...

9.   Write a personal mission statement.

10.   Pray - Meditate - Connect to your higher power.

11.   Recall your favorite subject in school.

12.   Learn something new.

13.   Create your own personal board of directors.

14.   Visualize your authentic life.

The Sankofa bird is characterized by turning its head in the direction of its tail. In reality, the bird is either removing something from its tail, searching through its tail feathers, or grooming itself. The Akan of Western Africa make up one of the largest ethnic/cultural groups inhabiting Ghana and the Ivory Coast. They liken this action to looking backward, a symbol of looking at one's past, or with the quest for knowledge, returning to the source. Looking back in order to move forward empowers you to discover your authenticity, affirm your talents, and own your power.

Looking back to discover your authentic core values, attributes, and skills in order to demonstrate them in the organization will empower and ensure you that you are seen as valuable to the organization.

Authenticity is discovering your core values. Organizations depend on employees conforming to the organization's core values. Core values may appear in a corporate manual or, many times, core values are the guiding principles of the company.

Core values are the guiding principles that you live by. Guiding principles help you to make difficult decisions or communicate what is important to you. Examples include fairness, honesty, integrity, security, or empathy. Core values typically originate from your life experiences. Think of a time in your life when you were faced with an

opportunity to work on a team in high school. It doesn't
matter what kind of team, what is important is that the
team's core values, or guiding norms, are congruent with
what you hold as important to you. Deep inside, when
trying to decide if joining the team works for you, it will
depend on how you feel about the team's core values. If
the team's core value is winning at all costs this may be a
problem for you because "at all costs" may mean
overlooking the need for being fair, which is a core value
for you.

"The road to happiness lies in two simple principles: Find what it is that interests you and that you can do well, and when you find it put your whole soul into it- every bit of energy and ambition and natural ability you have." **John D. Rockefeller**

Chapter 8 - You Are More Than Your Résumé:

How to Increase Job Security

No one really knows when the economy will change for the better. All we know right now is we must find ways to survive as millions are laid off and uncertainty looms.

Job insecurity is affecting how people work. Employers are challenging employees to move beyond the basic job requirements. As budget cuts are a daily concern, employers are trying to find ways to rationalize who is laid off and who should remain at work. When making these difficult decisions, employers focus on the company's profit margin and the perceived value of each employee.

Workers are striving to find ways to remain indispensable and to find strengths that create a competitive edge to set themselves apart from other employees.

What is Your Competitive Edge?

Finding your authentic strength in the workplace goes beyond what appears on your résumé. Most of the skills listed on your résumé probably required training or education of some sort. Authentic strengths are innate qualities — they make up who you are, your "true self." In the *Psychology Today* article "In Search of the Real You"

(2000), Michael Kernis and Brian Goodman, graduate students at the University of Georgia, discuss a technical definition for "authentic." They call it "the unimpeded operation of one's true or core self in one's daily enterprise."

Natural talents and gifts exist inside each of us to make us who we are. Finding our core skills is like going on an archaeological self-exploration.

Looking beyond your résumé, what strengths can you demonstrate that exhibit passion with minimum effort?

The job market demands continuous self-exploration to help maintain a sense of empowerment. Kernis and Goldman found that a sense of authenticity has many benefits – people who score high on the authenticity profile are more likely to respond to difficulties with effective coping strategies.

What is your authentic profile? Have you demonstrated hidden talents and skills that would impact productivity? Are you visibly demonstrating additional strengths in the workplace? Have you volunteered to get out of your comfort zone to create opportunities that demonstrate that you are more than your job description?

Part II

"Funthentic" Tips to Find Your Natural Strengths

Funthentic Tip #1 – Talk to Close Friends

Find friends from middle school or high school that knew you well – you know, friends that you hung out with at parties, shopping, after-school activities or were with you at school activities. Find these old friends, even if you have not talked with them in years. This is the fun part because this could be a mini high school reunion – the event you put off doing for a number of years.

Meet for lunch or dinner. Food seems to be a common denominator for good conversation with good friends. Open up with reconnecting time – not too long you don't want to miss the opportunity to accomplish your goal – investigating key clues about your strengths.

It is important to create an informal atmosphere that is congruent to the group's normal behavior with a sense of seriousness. Allow your friends to understand that your reason to bring them together is to help you rediscover yourself, and that this is important to you. Select the place to meet. Great restaurants always work. Or, create a home-cooked meal (I took a risk in getting my old friends together to create this meeting for me. But I felt my journey to discovering me was worth the risk. Besides, this was a good reason to reconnect.)

Here's the script for people you have not spoken to in a long time.

"Hi,

I know we have not talked in a long time.

How are you? Yada yada yada … What have you been doing, etc.?

I would like to reconnect with you for lunch or dinner sometime soon, not only to have a fun time, but also because I am working on creating my next career and I think you could really help me."

Here's a script for people with whom you've kept in contact.

"Hi,

I need to meet with you for lunch or dinner. I am working on creating my next career and I need your help."

At the get-together ask your friends this question: "What was I doing in high school/middle school that appeared effortless, and like I was having fun?"

Listen to the conversation carefully. Listen for clues when your friends describe your natural strengths and talents. This upbeat conversation is contagious – you may find your friends wanting to key in on their own rediscovery conversation. Gently, try to keep the focus on you and remind your friends why you asked them to reconnect/connect with you.

When I connected with my friends I did not know what to expect. I was a little nervous about how they would describe what I had done in school. One of my friends, much to my surprise, reminded me that I was always volunteering to be in the school plays. She said I looked happy during these plays and would always make friends come and see me. I picked up on the clue about what I loved doing. I followed up with my "silver clue" and signed up for an acting class. My first acting class was a revelation for me. I actually enjoyed what I was doing. Any added joy in my life was a bonus and I stayed with the class to the end. That was almost five years ago. Today I enjoy acting in television commercials and model for print. I was blessed to rediscover a part of my authentic self through this process.

Remember

- Ask your friends to give only positive feedback. Say, "I want our conversation to be fun."

- This is not a therapy session. "No solving problems."

- Keep the conversation focused on the mission, then let your friends join the sharing session. (This may sound self-serving, but it is very easy to get distracted, especially when you have not seen the friends in a long time.)

- Spend only one hour on your issues. (You do not want your friends to think the entire meeting is about you.)

- Listen for the clues to who you are.

- Investigate one clue; revisit the experience – be curious about what you will discover about your "true self."

- Follow through and rediscover the joy.

- Celebrate your inner work.

Funthentic Tip #2 – If You Don't Have a Group, Talk to a Friend

Select a close friend or family member who has known you for a significant amount of time to identify a positive skill or trait that you demonstrated with ease, and you exhibited joy while doing.

Someone you trust could be a colleague or friend, but "trust" means that you receive honest and positive feedback using constructive communication. This should be someone who is really your champion and wants you to be the best that you can be. Select someone who engages you in conversation that helps you create an image of your strength — something that you did that was as easy as breathing.

By asking someone who has been your companion in life to help you find your authentic self, you can surface the part of yourself that is a natural state of who you are. This is often a part of yourself that you take for granted. Ask someone you talk to often, who is able to give you genuine feedback.

Someone you trust may have observed you for a long period of time, but you've never had an opportunity to talk about your positive skills and traits with this person. Many times we take these close relationships for granted and don't realize that the person who knows you is holding a lot of information about you that you never seem to talk about.

Many times, unfortunately, close friends will pick out our negative traits trying to help us to improve, but seldom do we get a chance to exchange what is positive about what we do well – our strengths and what comes easy to us. This is very important. When you talk to someone you trust, he or she may ask you, "How do I know what

you are doing that comes as easy to you as breathing?"
Well, you can say, "When I'm demonstrating a strength, it
looks easy and I'm having a great time or I am filled with
joy."

For example, a friend of mine loves to cook, and
one day I was watching her prepare a meal. She just
looked like she was having fun. She enjoyed picking out
the different flavors and spices, she knew what pots to use
to cook the food, and most of all; she was talking
constantly while she was in the kitchen. I said, "You know
you look like you can cook this meal with your eyes
closed." She laughed, and said, "I've been cooking most of
my life, cooking comes easy to me. I watched my mother
cook, and for some reason, I just seem to know how much
of an ingredient to put in without looking at a cookbook."
She said she doesn't stress about cooking — it's not about
making it perfect. Her cooking is about bringing out the
good flavors that people would enjoy. She enjoys cooking
because it brings happiness to her when people say her food
tastes delicious. Cooking was also like therapy for her: It's
relaxing.

Remember

- Listen for clues in the conversation (i.e. - remember how you loved to organize events).

- Investigate a "silver star" clue that heightens your curiosity to check if you can still do this activity with ease and with joy.

- Revisit the experience to see if it still brings you joy.

- Follow through and rediscover a part of your authentic self — the "true" you. You may be surprised what you will find.

- Celebrate your inner work.

Funthentic Tip # 3 – Identify Core Values

Core values are your beliefs – what is important to you? Core values build the foundation for being authentic. Along the way in your rediscovering process you will encounter past situations that surface beliefs that helped you survive or made you stronger.

Integrity is on the top of my core value list. When I am faced with a situation that impacts my integrity, an emotional warning light is triggered. This means I need to either say something to someone or act on something. This feeling will not go away until I do something.

Here's an exercise to discover your core values. Write down five core values based on your life stories — in your work or personal life. In your personal life with your family, think of situations when in your gut you knew something was not right. That situation caused you to stop and think about why this is constantly on your mind. What belief is surfacing in you? Honesty is a core value for many people. Honesty is my second top core value.

My top core value — integrity — was tested while working as a Human Resource Change Management Consultant for a financial services company. A friend suggested that I apply for an opening at a college in Philadelphia — senior vice president of organizational development. I was hesitant about applying for the position based on issues with race and gender I heard were playing out at this particular school. I was also hesitant due to the situation of an upcoming layoff of employees at my current place of work. I planned to take advantage of the merger and teach at a university in the area. However, I finally decided to apply for the position. I found out that 200 people were applying for it, and I knew the interview process was going to be challenging.

I tend to follow my intuition when making difficult decisions or moving through an experience that can impact my life. In the initial application process I was in a place of "well, let's see what happens." Several people I knew who worked at the school were encouraging me to apply. Little did I know that the "pinches" I was feeling in my gut about working at the school would come to fruition. Pinches are my way of identifying something that I feel intuitively. I typically characterize these feelings as "pinches" – something feels uncomfortable – or "Aha! moments" – something feels good or I am having a wonderful learning moment. I use the term "pinches" to express what I'm feeling and I decided to observe the experience.

I handed in my application and several weeks later I received a phone call from the Human Resources office at the school. The person on the phone acknowledged receiving my application and requested 10 references. I thought I was hearing things – 10 references? I am accustomed to submitting three or, at maximum, five references. The response from the hiring manager was that due to the high-level position, 10 references were required. Pinch #1.

A month passed after that initial phone call and when I received a call from a friend who I submitted as one of the 10 references for my application. He asked whether I was applying for the job of president of the university. When I asked why, this friend told me that the Human Resources firm kept him on the phone for two hours asking questions about me. I laughed, because I could sense from the beginning that this organization was trying to find out if I can walk on water. Pinch #2.

Two more months passed. One day I was wondering about the hiring process; due to the length of time it was taking to narrow down applicants. I received a call from the hiring manager congratulating me that they narrowed down the applicants and I was one of 20 to begin the interview process. I was pleased with the results of this phase of the interview. I felt proud that my organizational development skills paid off.

The initial interview was with the hiring manager – a woman who worked there for a number of years and was delighted that I was one of 20 in the interview process. During the interview I felt a sense of urgency in finding someone to fill the position. The climate in the organization during that time was a state of massive reorganization. She expressed a need to hire someone who had experience in working with organizations during change, including a new president, disgruntled employees, and low morale. I listened and, because my background is change management, I was interested even though I still had the feeling that I was not sure if this institution was congruent with my core values. She said she would get in touch with me with a final decision regarding the final phase of the interview process, which would include three candidates.

Two more months passed, and I did not think about the position. So much time had passed that I assumed I was not one of the final three candidates and they were taking their time notifying the interviewees. Keep in mind, I still had this gut feeling of not being sure if this is the place I wanted to be. I do not take my talents and skills for granted. I was grateful that I was one of 20 applicants being considered for the position. I try to take advantage of opportunities when they come to me. I felt a strong sense of "spirit" – God telling me to keep moving forward, there is a reason. It is difficult to explain how powerful this feeling was to stay in the interview process. I was calm and at the same time curious about the results – with three pinches already. I was curious. I was not creating a self-fulfilling prophecy about the results because I was always open to the idea that whatever happens, it is for a good reason.

One month later I received a phone call from the hiring manager. With a jubilant voice she said, "Barbara, congratulations – you are one of the final three candidates!" I was excited because I was close to becoming a senior vice president at a university. I felt elated and grateful that my talents, skills, and work experience were recognized. By this time, almost six months had passed since I had first applied – enough time to recover from my initial three pinches about interviewing for this position. The hiring manager gave me the time and place for the final interview. A friend at the university who recommended me for the position was one of five interviewers. I said to myself, "Well, this is great! Her belief and confidence in me can only help me in the interview."

I arrived at the office for the interview and was escorted to a conference room. A long counter against the wall with a sink and large faucets looked typical of rooms you might see in a laboratory and I thought, "Well, this is interesting. Maybe they did not have any rooms available for the interview." I sat waiting for almost 20 minutes – for me, waiting that long for someone does not feel good at all. I always pride myself in making sure I do not keep anyone waiting 20 minutes or longer for a meeting. Keeping someone waiting may communicate several messages, such as you are not that important and you can wait; you are here for a job, if you want it that bad you can wait; or the person who is keeping me waiting is feeling stressed and needs the time to get it together.

Anyway, the interviewer came in the room – it was someone in a senior-level position who apologized for keeping me waiting. He mentioned that he could not attend the final interview later because he had another meeting. This communicated to me that additional interviewers were on the agenda. No problem – this is customary when you get this far. Ten minutes into the meeting I heard a gurgling noise. I was sitting with my back to the sink. The noise got louder and then, in a matter of seconds, I felt cold water spouting out of the sink and spraying on top of me.

The interviewer apologized profusely while I was wiping my clothes, trying to find a towel. People came scurrying in from the hallway to see what all the noise was and someone finally brought me a paper towel. Yes, we did complete the interview with an embarrassed interviewer and me thinking, "OK, this is really Pinch #4, and I am still moving forward." Then I thought, "This seems more than a pinch; is this a sign of anything I need to pay attention to?" Of course, accidents happen and I got myself together and patiently waited for the final interview.

I was escorted to the next room feeling damp and wondering about the final interview. As I entered the room I saw five people – three Human Resources executives, the hiring manager, and one man recently hired as an employee relations manager. Everyone was polite and welcomed me and explained how the interview would proceed.

The questions did not sound like typical interview questions for a senior-level position – the questions were more like those you would ask a consultant who was working with a client to solve critical issues. In the back of my mind, I was thinking, "I should bill these people for picking my brain on Human Resources topics." After two hours of questioning, the Employee relations manager looked at me quizzically and asked in a serious tone, "How did you learn to speak in Standard English and be articulate?" His words resonated in my ear and I felt like was in a surreal moment. My body felt frozen inside; my thoughts were doing flips from anger to disbelief that someone would ask me this question in an interview. My credentials were public knowledge, and I could not have gotten this far without learning "basic English." He could not tell by the expression on my face what I was thinking because my grandmother always told me, "Never let anyone know what you are thinking when you are prepared to defend yourself." I remained calm and said in a quiet and firm voice, "I learned to speak Standard English like you did from what I learned in school and from my parents." My tone was not defensive – deep down inside anger was surfacing and it was difficult to complete the final moments in the interview.

I felt frustrated as a woman and an African American who was tired of hearing people say the stereotypical words "you are articulate" to me. This experience was a profound moment for me because of my role as a Human Resources organizational practitioner, training diversity initiatives for clients at a major financial institution. The term "accumulative impact" is used in diversity training as a model designed by Elsie Y. Cross, a well-known author and consultant, to describe the feeling of being negatively impacted by discrimination and stereotypical behavior over and over during a long period. In this experience, the negative impact of being asked the question – "How did you learn to speak Standard English?" – had passed a point of a rational explanation for what I was feeling. When I heard the interviewer's question I knew that accumulative impact was surfacing and my core value of integrity was kicking in and needed my attention.

It was evident to me, that the intent of the director of employee relations' comments to me was not based on hate, but on ignorance. His stereotypical comments I assume came from his life experiences or lack of experiences in dealing with women and people of color.

After the interview I asked the hiring manager whether she noticed anything offensive in the interview. She said, "This is typical in this culture at the university." I was surprised at her response and immediately I had flashbacks to the "pinches" I felt in the interview process. I was angry and disappointed that the interview ended with a negative tone. I could not sleep for several nights – I knew I had to make a difficult decision whether to continue with the interview because of the feeling of "accumulative impact" and the strong feeling of my value about being who I am – knowing that demonstrating integrity is key to my authentic self. *Psychology Today* magazine mentions in the article *"Dare To Be Yourself,"(Psychology Today –* June 2008) the pain of authenticity. The article mentions a potential downside to authenticity – accurate self-knowledge can be painful. It also mentions that "behaving in accord with your true self may also bring on the disfavor of others."

Some of my colleagues could not understand why I was getting upset about an interview comment when I was a viable candidate for the position. The researchers in the article *"Dare to Be Yourself"* (June 2008), Kernis and Goldman observe, it can feel better to be embraced as an impostor than dumped for the person you really are. Fortunately, my diversity training peers supported me in my reaction to the interview. They helped me to process my feelings and make a decision on what I wanted to do and what I needed from the university. I decided to write a letter stating that I could no longer continue with the interview process because I did not feel the university was a place where I would feel emotionally safe to work and work competently. I suggested a more effective way for the university to use my skills would be to hire me as a consultant to design an organizational initiative to help employees value and manage differences in the university. I thought instead of pointing blame at the hiring manager, I wanted to suggest how I could use my experience to help the university.

Due to my background in diversity consulting, I knew that stereotyping comments surface from a lack of knowledge, cultural upbringing, the media, and, unfortunately, ignorance. My anger was triggered by my core value of integrity. My belief is that every human being deserves to be treated with respect and that we should all value each other's differences.

I had mixed emotions after the final interview because I felt that the interview process caused a financial loss for the university and I wanted an opportunity to use my skills for organizational change. However, sometimes in life you must face the reality of what is more important – being true to self or trying to please people. When your core value is being challenged the voice does not go away. I did not want to keep thinking if I accepted the position that I sold out instead of being who I am. You might be thinking, "Well, Barbara, this happens in organizations and you should get over it as a woman and an African American." Well, it is easy to think this except for one thing —I was being true to who I am and focusing on my critical core value 'integrity."

The following week I received a phone call from the hiring manager. The letter I had written was on my desk ready to mail with several blind copies to various individuals at the university. I told the hiring manager my decision. She was shocked and irate. I was disappointed that she did not understand the reason for my decision.

However, when I ended the conversation, thanking her for her time, I felt a sense of relief that I was being authentic and true to me. Sometimes, difficult life decisions appear to help us develop character and to know ourselves better than anyone could ever understand.

Remember

- Brainstorm core values – think about past stories about your life. Try to recall situations that challenged your character or a difficult decision you had to make.

- Write down five core values or beliefs about you, life, people, or success.

- Prioritize your core values – these may change as you grow.

- Keep your core values somewhere close by to remind you who you are.

Funthentic Tip # 4 – Get Out of Your Comfort Zone

"Everybody thinks of changing humanity and nobody thinks of changing himself." — Leo Tolstoy

Getting out of your comfort zone means experiencing life as though it were an adventure to discover more about you. It is the archaeological dig that helps you discover who you are, with added excitement to the process. These activities will challenge you to reveal hidden talents.

Stretch yourself to experiment with new activities, such as something you always thought about doing, but were afraid to try. This career-empowerment strategy helps to peel off another layer in discovering who you are.

For example, you may discover in meeting with old friends that you are good at roller-skating. Now this may not lead to a career choice, but it does give you an added feeling of accomplishment. If you remembered that you enjoyed hiking, group travel tours are great for opening up to new experiences and connecting to a passion. Or you could try spelunking, an adventure that put me way out of my comfort zone.

After you hear of your skills and talents you may have forgotten about, it's time to test the waters of discovery.

"Discovering your authenticity" means getting out of your comfort zone and pushing the envelope to make something different happen in your life.   Denzel Washington quoted his wife Pauline at his commencement speech at the University of Pennsylvania stating, "To get something you've never had, you have to do something you've never done."

I enrolled in a master's degree program during the late 1970s that required taking an advanced group analysis course. I recalled this story years later because it impacted my life by uncovering new information about me.

This two-week course in Bushkill, predominantly a forest and bush area in the Pennsylvania mountains, was conducted by a young professor fresh out of graduate school. He explained that the course was designed to teach physical intervention strategies for doing group process work. The purpose of this activity was to assess our leadership styles and to analyze how groups function and interact with each other.

As I was unfamiliar with the terminology, a classmate whispered that we were going cave climbing. I knew this was going to be an adventure that would really stretch my comfort zone.

For three days, all I thought about was the cave. My emotions were mixed with concern, fear and excitement. The day arrived and, after donning my spelunking gear, I felt like I was going on a safari. The professor provided little information about the trip.

I kept thinking to myself that there must be another way to get through this course. Did I really pay all this money just to go through a cave? En route to the cavern, our instructor showed us a beautiful waterfall. At the bottom were cold cans of refreshing beer and soda. "This is what will be waiting for us after we have completed our quest," he said.

I remember staying close to my classmate, Fred, because he was 6 feet tall and had a protective look I thought I would need in the cave. He proved to be a wonderful partner.

The cave felt cold and damp. It was dark inside and crawling was a challenge. I could barely hold my head up at times. And, at one point, I could not see my hand in front of me. The group helped and supported each other, but emotions escalated as we inched through the cave.

At first, I was not the model student. Once inside the cave, I fussed and complained that I did not want to be here. It was dark, wet, and very hot, and I know I saw a few bats flying around my head. I kept asking myself, "Why am I doing this?"

After a few hours in the cave, we stopped at an open area that was very dark. The instructor asked the group to express their feelings. I suddenly realized that classmates were revealing many sides of themselves that I had not detected from prior program courses. When faced with a challenge, it is amazing what thoughts come to mind. I remember thinking about my children, and how much they depended on me to prepare them for young adulthood.

Although we followed instructions and were determined to complete the experience, some of us were ready to form a mutiny by the fifth hour in the cave. There I was with 20 strangers, wondering out loud why I had paid such high tuition for the course. These comments were mild compared to those expressed by my colleagues.

As I climbed through the cave, many times on my stomach, there was another woman in front of me. Behind me was the classmate who stood more than 6 feet tall. He comforted me in the beginning, when I was feeling unsure and did not believe we would every get out of the cave.

Surprisingly, as I began to follow the group, I felt no fear. Rather, I felt confident that we were, in fact, getting out of this cave. I trusted those around me, and even offered to help others who needed assistance. While climbing, I was focused on helping those people deal with their fear and frustration. Before going in the cave, certain people in the group were experiencing some tension relating to each other. Gender, race, or other issues created barriers to communication. In the cave, misperceptions were broken down quickly.

Our instructor guided us through and remained at the end of the line on our way back out. While crawling out, someone suggested that we return without light. I supported the challenge, being caught up in the moment. I wanted to see if we could really do this.

This challenge, however, was not well accepted by one group member. As the group moved on, she yelled, "I refuse to climb any further without any light."

We were all exhausted and wanted to get out of the cave. Our instructor took advantage of this time to process our decisions within the group. I noticed that we had begun to challenge him and push the boundaries within the group as we became more comfortable and trusting of each other. Most of us weren't sure what to do because we could not move. We participated in an interactive group discussion in the cave anyway.

The result of our discussion was to use light as we returned. Moreover, the current leader in the cave decided that she did not want to lead anymore; so, the group asked for volunteers. Guess who volunteered? Yes, I did. Why I did, I now understand.

After five hours, we emerged from the cave successfully. After several discussions in the cave, and with group support, we succeeded in meeting our goal.

As we ended our long, hot, and scary journey out of the dark, we found the beer, soda and all the food that we could eat. We were all so thrilled that we made it out that we became stronger. We were patting each other on the backs and hugging. One group member said, "Hey, Barbara, I knew you could lead us out. You were great." Everyone verbalized their confidence in my leading them out safely.

I appreciated everyone's comments, but I knew we worked together as a team, supporting each other. Leading out of the cave was my choice to help us achieve our goal.

The group's vote of confidence impacted me. Internalizing my emotions, I sat alone on a rock and tried to process my feelings. David[1], my instructor, came over and asked what was going on with me. He commented on my excellent leadership skills and assumed that I would feel

---

[1] Name has been changed for the sake of privacy.

good about my role in our adventure. I explained that although I felt supported by the group, I felt I was being taken for granted.

He reinforced how I had helped and supported those people who felt lost. He noted how everyone was expressing grateful feelings toward me. I believed everyone was congratulating me because they expected me to be strong. I volunteered because no one else would.

I needed just as much validation as anyone else in our group. He asked how much more validation I needed, and we continued to talk. David helped me to understand something about myself. He told me that people created perceptions about me based on what they saw and their own experiences. What people see is their reality.

He said, "Your group saw you as a strong leader. Did you want them to see you any other way? Yes, of course, you were afraid, but you were also courageous. Why don't you want people to see your strength? Maybe you have difficulty in owning your power.

You demonstrated power and communicated leadership, but you want people to see something in you that is not true. You want others to sympathize with you."

That statement hit me hard.

What I learned many years later from that cave experience is that to be authentic means to acknowledge the gift of leadership and power that God has given me. I need to be what people see in me. This is being authentic.

I asked myself why I needed people to see me as fearful rather than courageous and strong. Many years later, I recalled that experience. I remembered that I was going through a difficult divorce, raising two daughters and completing my master's degree while working a full-time job. Deep inside, I wanted people to feel sorry for me. It was hard to admit that I did not own my power. My instructor's words stung; but going through that experience brought to the surface information about me that I may not have known. What I did learn later in life was that I am strong, courageous, and not afraid to take risks. Yes, leading the group through the cave was challenging; but I needed affirmation that could only come from within me.

Years after the spelunking experience, I ran into my instructor and reminded him about the cave. He laughed and remarked, "Don't remind me; I was a bit too adventurous as a young professor."

The cave experience is a physical intervention strategy designed to challenge groups to process group dynamics, and many times, it brings out deep interpersonal issues in group members that create life-changing experiences. You may not want to go spelunking, but I'm sure you can find an enjoyable physical activity that gets you out of your comfort zone, something you can do with friends or strangers, that challenges you to surface the gems buried inside of you.

After one of my workshops, a woman shared her experience about her trip to the Amazon River. I was impressed with her interest in spending time in a place that most people find challenging. She said the trip validated that she is more than she thinks she is. Proving her authenticity about strength and purpose was her greatest reward. Prior to the trip, she said she had forgotten that she was strong. But the Amazon was the place she would have to depend on for survival to find herself again. As a result, she looks at challenges differently today.

Taking a trek to the Amazon may not be your idea of empowerment, but adventure empowerment strategies challenge you to reach deep down inside, connecting you to your inner strength and values. Getting out of your comfort zone may add on another layer to affirm who you are in this world and your purpose in life.

In my travels, I meet men and women who want contentment and happiness in life. I read somewhere that life is what you make it and only you can make what you want to happen. Prior to my journey to empowerment, I resented the fact that no one was going to rescue me and change my world. I realized that changing was going to be my responsibility. Getting out of my comfort zone began to free me from the past.

Remember

- Select a place, activity or event that creates some anxiety - not a feeling of being out of control.

- You have control over the something that makes you feel physically and emotionally safe. You can make healthy choices as to where to go and what to do.

- The anxiety you feel is fear of the unknown. Do your homework - find the information you need to help you move through the fear.

- Be clear about your intention – ask yourself why are you doing this; do you want to test your skills, discover your inner strength; discover your natural strengths? There could be other reasons you may need for clarity.

- Remember getting out of your comfort zone is something you decided to do for yourself - you're taking responsibility for your own self-discovery journey

Funthentic Tip #5 – Write Your Life Story

Writing your life story may seem like a daunting experience – like, "Where do I begin?" Negative thoughts such as, "Who would be interested in reading about me?" should be pushed away. The life story is not written for someone to read, the life story writing is to help lift out positive information about yourself that maybe you forgot.

My life story began with my first book – I wrote my book initially to document my career journey. At first it seemed easy until I realized that what was most important was to include my life stories. Your life story does not have to lead to a book; however, the information you discover in your life story can lead to the beginning of an authentic and transformational life.

Your life story reveals information about who you are – and an opportunity to recapture events and experiences that were taken for granted.

Your life story is the blueprint for who you are. We are influenced and molded by what we experience in life. Generally, what happens is we live the stories then move onto the next story. We live each moment of our lives because sometimes the experience is too painful to recapture or remember. How about if we recalled our life stories that described the authentic part of who we are?

One of my life stories regarding why I became a teacher begins with me as a 9-year-old. My mother sent me to a wonderful Salvation Army Camp named Star Lake Camp. My mother, aunts, and cousins all went to this camp – I guess going to Star Lake Camp was like a rite of passage in my family. I loved summer camp because we lived in the projects in the Bronx, N.Y. When I first arrived at camp I remember entering a place filled with wonderful trees. I did not see trees in the Bronx. These trees were tall and very green. Then, as we drove up a hill, I looked out a window and saw the most beautiful lake. There were no lakes in the Bronx, so I was amazed at the sight of water. I remember my mother showing me pictures of Star Lake Camp with her standing on the deck beside the lake.

My camp experience taught me how much I loved playing with children from all over New York State. We all had a common experience of attending a Salvation Army Church in our neighborhood. Some of us had parents and grandparents who were Salvation Army officers. My grandparents, Majors Lambert and Estava Bailey, were officers of the African American Salvation Army and pastored a church in Harlem, N.Y. I was used to the songs we sang and at night hearing the beautiful sounds of the bands. Salvation Army churches always had wonderful brass bands playing beautiful songs.

When I turned 13, I qualified to become a junior counselor. I couldn't wait to be a counselor at camp because I learned to appreciate helping my friends and teaching the younger campers about nature, arts and crafts, and helping their counselors get them ready for bed. I was excited to begin working and teaching children younger than me. I felt like a big girl – I was going to receive my first paycheck.

My first job as a junior counselor was exciting. The campers called me "Miss Barbara." My job was to help the senior counselors with their assigned campers. I assisted the campers in getting dressed, with their classes, and even got to sit at the head of the table with the senior counselor at the opposite end of the table. I was a junior counselor for three years. When I turned 16, I became a senior counselor. My love for working with children began at Star Lake Camp. I knew I wanted to be a teacher. Remembering my camping experience helped me to understand my natural strengths in teaching. I attended one of the best teacher's colleges – Cheyney State College in Pennsylvania, now called Cheyney State University – and became a fourth-grade teacher.

Western philosopher Socrates believed that an unexamined life is not worth living, but he left out information about what that really means. Karen Wright in her article *"Dare to be Yourself – the 8 Rules for Authentic Living,"* believed we discover authenticity, "the existentialists say we invent it." I think an unexamined life leaves missing gaps of precious information that validates who you are and natural talents and gifts you bring to the world.

Writing a life story is for the courageous; it is for anyone who believes that what he will find will be worth it because the information will propel him into another world of "knowing."

Writing a life story means accepting unconditionally whatever you will find with love of yourself. The "silver star clue" is knowing you did not come into this world with a blank slate – knowing and affirming "that you are more than you think you are." And that's the truth!

Healing can also be a benefit in writing your life stories. These are stories that helped you learn a few hard life lessons, and they can help you recognize your survival skills, especially if you are experiencing midlife, which today can be between the ages of 40 and 65.

Write your life story with vigor and with a feeling of deservedness – I am not sure if this is a real word, but it fits for what I mean. Write your life story with the same energy as you would when telling someone about your true self.

What exactly should you write in your life story?

These are opening ideas. Not all are required to write a life story, but this is a way to get warmed up to begin sharing what you know is true. This is about how you got to be who you are today.

- When you were born?

- Where did you live most of your life?

- What was your family structure?

- What schools did you attend?

- What did you like doing in school? Is there a life story from school that you can say impacted you?

- What activity brought you joy, fun, excitement?

- What were you good at doing?

- What came easy to you?

Who was your favorite teacher? (This is a "silver star clue" because your favorite teacher can give you insights to your special qualities. Typically a favorite teacher is someone who liked you, a lot. He or she was your favorite because you were a person to this teacher. You were acknowledged by this teacher. Your story about your relationship with this teacher may offer an opportunity to see yourself thorough someone else's lens. Be specific about comments that your teacher made about you – what did the teacher teach you about certain subjects that were interesting to you in class? Why did this teacher spark your interest?)

Who inspired you as a role model? What life story depicts "silver star clues" that you learned from your role model?

Write about a challenging time in your life and how you overcame the adversity. What transformation did you experience?

When and where you were born? Your culture moves with you toward adulthood, and many times surfaces when making decisions, where you live, or even your choice of friends.

What do you remember about growing up in your family – this is not a therapeutic process to assess any painful memories about family issues, try to focus on what YOU did growing up that gave you joy, a respite from survival, what you did to decrease stress, what you did in your family that everyone counted on you to do because you did it well (baked the best cake or cookies – whatever you were always asked to do.) This is critically important because this will give you insights on who you are and what came easy to you.

What were you doing in school? Write a biography of things that you were doing that demonstrated a talent or skill. Caution that you do not minimize what you were doing as not important. It is important to you!

What were you doing in your neighborhood with your friends? Document games you played in which you excelled. I was one of the best double jumpers on my street – why is this important? This gave me information that I was good at something that was physical and energetic. I can still jump double-dutch rope – well, maybe not as fast as when I was a young child, but I can still feel the joy!

My love of acting and performing today began when I was 9-years-old. I stayed home alone when I had a mild cold. I remember my mother saying she could not stay home with me because she had to work. She made sure my cold was not serious enough to take me to the doctor. During that time society was not filled with the fears of leaving children at home alone. Many baby boomers were called "latch-key kids" because our parents had to work and we would use our house keys to let ourselves in our homes after school. I wanted to keep myself occupied because there weren't many television channels to watch anything that was fun. I remember vividly cutting pictures out of magazines of famous actors and actresses and writing fan mail to my favorite star. I was obsessed with movies and acting. I would go to the movies every Saturday with my friends. Loving to connect with acting at a young age was a huge "silver star clue" about what brings me joy.

I remember the story I mentioned in my first book *"It's Your Turn: Find Your Authentic Self and Go Fetch It!"* – my high school friends reminded me how much I loved performing in our school plays. After recalling my love of acting, I took acting lessons as an adult. Today I make money from acting and modeling in film and print commercials.

Writing your life story is a wonderful way to rediscover or discover what life events impact you still today.

Writing your life story is an opportunity to take a moment to reflect on your talents and gifts. A life story is not a biography. Writing a life story is like writing a series of essays about experiences that give you "silver star clues" about your authentic self.

After you write your life story it is helpful to read the story out loud to yourself. There is something about hearing words that describe your experience. You may need to read your life story several times in order for the experience to sink in.

Your life story is precious evidence of you. Treat the words with love. If sadness surfaces, embrace the feeling – this means you are human. Don't labor the pain – move on and remember you are searching for your core beliefs. Sometimes our core values surface after we experience adversity. Celebrate the joyful parts of your story – core beliefs can surface from happy experiences. Whatever you discover after you write your story, you may want to share this with a friend or family member. Whatever you decide is fine because this is YOUR story.

Remember

- Select a quiet time to write – without distractions.

- You can write in a journal or a notepad.

- Write in increments, and take your time. Use maybe 15 minutes each day, or if you are the type that loves to write, select a longer period of time.

- The story does not have to be perfect. Remember, this is for you to reflect and rediscover who you are.

- Read, reflect, remember, and recall your authentic self. Look for clues for your natural strengths and your core beliefs.

Funthentic Tip #6 – Get Help if You Need it

Seeking therapy or counseling can be uncomfortable for some people. In some cultures, seeking therapy is seen as being weak. I tend to believe that asking an expert to help you create a strong beginning for self-discovery is a good thing. Therapy helped me to learn how to give myself love and compassion and realize that I deserve to find the true me that I know is good.

Seek a therapist if you need to find the courage to strengthen your self-esteem before you embark on rediscovering your authentic self. Many people tend to avoid seeing a therapist because they are fearful of what they may discover about themselves – they want to avoid the negative perception of being "crazy." Therapy may help you understand the blocks that may surface when you begin to find out who you are. In my journey and transformation I needed to believe that I deserved to find my authenticity to create a better life. A therapist helped me to work through issues of doubt and insecurity in moving forward to rediscover or discover the real me.

Seeking a therapist is an important process. When you make the decision to seek help you first need to be clear about your intentions. I made it clear that a therapist would walk me through the process of revealing parts of me that I forgot – I needed support because the idea of searching more about me was not what I was used to doing in my life. I questioned the fear that came up every time I thought about going on this archaeological dig of rediscovering the good about me. A therapist helped me to move through the fear in order to do the work needed to capture the "golden nuggets" about who I am.

The first task she asked me to do was to buy myself flowers. This was a daunting exercise for me because my life was focused on teaching, raising my two daughters, and always doing for others. It seemed like there was never enough time for me. I made excuses about why I could not take a break from the day. Buy flowers? I did not see the point in this task or how it would help me on my inner journey to discover my authentic self. My therapist said, "This task is not so much about the flowers, it is more about taking time to love yourself and realize that the true you is a woman who is loved by you." Love is a healing force and buying flowers connects to what I love – beautiful flowers. When I went to the flower shop I was amazed at all the beautiful colors and the different aromas. I believe this assignment was meant to be because when I began my inner journey I prayed to be open to "silver star clues" that would lead me more to my true self. Today, I keep a green vase in my kitchen that I fill with flowers consistently.

Now this task did not increase my income, but seeking a therapist helped me to write my life stories and fortified my inner journey with courage.

Remember

- Check with the American Psychological Association for a licensed therapist in your area.

- Interview several therapists to assess your comfort level with him or her in what you want to achieve.

- If you are afraid, this is normal – looking inward at ourselves is not for the faint of heart; however, the joy of knowing more about who you are is worth it.

- Look for "silver star clues" about who you are in your therapy process.

Funthentic Tip #7 Brainstorm – What Would You do if You Were Not Afraid?

I am sure you have heard this question many times on talk shows, on the radio, or maybe you attended a personal growth seminar. Believe it or not, asking this question begins the process of thinking about "what if." Once you ask this question it is amazing how you begin to imagine your life differently.

Removing the fear factor allows you to brainstorm ideas of how you want to live your authentic life based on a need to recapture a dream. Maybe you had this dream in your youth and maybe life kicked in and you were on autopilot and did not have time to even think about this question. Well, now you can. You have my permission to get a sheet of paper and begin the brainstorming session.

You do not have to share this with anyone. Once you begin writing down ideas, try not to edit your thoughts with, "Well, I know this one will not work." When I began to brainstorm ideas to begin my authentic journey – I wrote I would like to be a photographer. Now I wasn't thinking about if this came easy to me – the idea just seemed interesting and creative. Photography would give me a chance to learn something new. No one mentioned this skill in my conversations with friends – I wrote it down anyway because I was curious.

I followed my curiosity – I took a photography class. I love to look at beautiful photography – I discovered that taking good pictures means learning the technical aspects of photography, i.e. depth of field, etc. This was not for me. I took photography off my list. I learned to appreciate the skill of photography but I'm a "shoot and take person." I appreciated discovering more about who I am. Don't censor your list – keep writing and you never know what you might discover.

Remember

- Keep writing for as long as you can – until you run out of ideas.

- Don't stress if you cannot think of an idea – sit with it for a while and see what happens. Rest your brain and return later.

- Don't judge your ideas.

- Review your list and put it aside for a few days.

- Prioritize your list.

- Select your top three.

Select one idea from your list and write how would your life change, increase your income, improve your health, give you passion or joy? It is important to write down your thoughts because the reasons give you the courage to move forward. Moving through your fear means you have made a decision to conquer your fears.

Funthentic Tip #8 Listen to People That Say to You

"How did you do that?"

"You make it look easy!"

"You always make that work!"

"You are really good at what you do – no one here can do this like you!"

Listen to what people say to you. These are "silver star clues" that surface hidden talents and gifts. These are ways to begin your journey to self-discovery. Sometimes it is challenging to accept the good things that people say. People say what they observe about you at your place of employment or even socially. Observations about you are more than making conversation – people notice when someone is doing something great and wonder why it comes easier to you than someone else.

Deepak Chopra says you are in your "dharma" when you are doing your purpose in life – your truth and it feels timeless – hours go by and you are still doing what brings you joy.

When I am speaking to an audience I know I love what I am doing because there is a sense of fulfillment – it comes easy to me, and I could speak for hours. The feeling of knowing that I am helping someone brings a sense of knowing who I am and this feels like my purpose in life. No one taught me how to speak. I came into this world with the gift of speaking, which I inherited in my genes from my grandmother and mother.

My grandmother was a wonderful orator. Because she and my grandfather were pastors in the Salvation Army Church, many times I witnessed my grandmother leading the congregation in prayer. She had a way with words and always engaged me in conversations while I watched her cook delicious West Indian dinners. She would always share with me her love for God. My grandfather was also a great speaker – I remember how strong he seemed standing in front of the church. People would respond to his words of wisdom.

My mother was also a great speaker. I had many opportunities to hear her speak because she was active in many organizations. She was not only a great speaker; she was a great writer and singer. When she was director of patient services and activities in a nursing home I would visit and watch how she motivated the patients to sing or talk about their lives. Of course, we all experience challenges in family relationships. I chose to focus on the natural strengths and skills that are in my family. This information helped me to identify my natural gifts in my authentic journey.

I listen to people describe what I do that say I do it well. I hold onto these descriptions and acknowledge this is who I am.

Listening to others talk about ourselves requires an attitude of strong acceptance of who we are. Taking in the truth that what you do is part of who you are is a gift of self-discovery.

Remember

- Take a mental note when someone says "how did you do that"? These are silver clues about who you are – your natural strengths.

- Be aware when you are doing something that brings you joy or satisfaction and the time passes quickly say, "Um...this is interesting – this may be a silver star clue."

- Review your "life story" (see Funthentic Tip #5). Try to find a silver clue in your story that describes what comes easy to you.

Again, a reminder, you did not come into this world with a blank slate in your DNA. Keep digging – keep rediscovering.

Funthentic Tip #9 – Write a Personal Mission Statement

A mission statement communicates your purpose in life – it's like a road map for your life. I wrote my mission statement many years ago.

"I want to live each day in gratitude; knowing that each day is a gift. I focus on healthy eating, exercising and thinking positive. Each day brings wonderful opportunities to acknowledge the love within myself, be a better person, giving and loving to my family and friends. My life will demonstrate my authentic self by fulfilling my mission that creates success in my work."

There are numerous books that can help you write a mission statement. The reason why I suggest a mission statement to find your authentic self is because it is a way to begin thinking about who you are. Writing your life purpose gets your attention about what you do well. You may not know the answer – thinking about you is good start. Your mission statement is not final – it can change depending on where you are in life. A mission statement includes the what, why, how and when. Most successful corporations have a mission statement to guide the organization to achieve goals. Thinking about where you are going helps you get where you want to go in life. The brain is an amazing organ – I think sometimes we underestimate the power of our thoughts. Writing a mission statement is the physical mechanism in our brain that helps design your best life.

Remember

- Don't force yourself to write a mission statement. You might want to work on this tip when you have completed one or two tips

- Save the mission statement as a draft and keep coming back to it when it is clear to you.

- Responding to the "why" communicates your intention.

- A mission statement is a life goal based on core values not performance or activity goals. The words communicate the person you want to be, your purpose in life or how you want to live your life.

Funthentic Tip #10 - Pray – Meditate – Connect to Your Higher Power

Creating a time to meditate is important in helping me acknowledge that there is a higher power where I go to find me and deal with the challenges of the day. Find what works for you to connect to your higher power and ask for guidance to knowing your truth.

I am a Christian and I believe in the power of prayer. I took a course in *Mindfulness Meditation – The Stress Reduction Program* at Jefferson Hospital Myrna Brind Center of Integrative Medicine, in Philadelphia, PA. There are different types of meditations; Mindful Meditation helps me to be in the moment and be still. My life can be quite hectic at times, and meditation slows down my pace to help me listen to the whisper in my ear – I choose to say it is Gods' voice speaking to me.

When I am still – I give my brain and my ear quiet time. I shut down the noise of distractions. I focus on me; I reflect on my experiences, my self-discovery journey in the moment. Meditation is a gift I give to myself so I can hear God.

I heard Dr. Maya Angelou speak in one of her presentations, that we all should take a "human" or a "mental health" day. Dr. Angelou encouraged the audience to take a personal day for ourselves. Go away for a day – maybe to a hotel where there are no distractions with phones. You will need discipline to not turn on the television. Go to a park or someplace quiet. Our minds needs to rest at least once a month. I went on a three day silent retreat. I could hear my brain saying, "Thank you."

How can you know where you are going if you are not listening? You are on this earth for a reason and hearing the whispers or feeling the nudges of why you are here are gifts to your soul.

Remember

- Give yourself permission to have a mental rest.

- Enjoy being in the moment – between every breath is God.

- Listen for the "silver clues."

Funthentic Tip #11 – Recall Your Favorite Subject in School

Try to remember course(s) in school that came easy to you or kept your attention, even if you have to rewind far back into your youth. I know, for many people school may not have been a positive experience; however, the most important part of this task is for you to recall your interests in school because there is a "silver star clue" hidden in this experience.

If you can, locate your favorite teacher – Ask to meet with him or her. She or he may not remember your name, but I assure you, if you were liked in class and contributed in class, and he or she singled you out for being a good student, you will be remembered.

Make an appointment and ask questions that will help you understand what came easy to you in class. Being a former teacher, I can recall specific ways I taught a specific subject and how special students performed in class. The information the teacher shares with you will help you learn about your natural gift that you brought to the class.

If the teacher you seek out does not remember you, then think about your experiences in school – elementary, middle school or high school, it does not matter. What is important is to recall what courses came easy to you. If your school experience was not positive because your teachers did not provide motivation to learn or you were not provided the home nurturing to support you in your learning experience; then think about if you could have removed all of the barriers to your learning – what subject areas would have grabbed your interest? Believe it or not, just recalling a spark saying, "You know, maybe if I had paid attention more or if I received more help in school then I think I would have liked art." Just the thought of saying, "I think I would have liked the art class or English class." Snatch that thought – freeze frame the thought and, as I say in my book, *"Go Fetch It!"* go fetch that "silver star" clue and begin seeking and asking yourself, "Why would I have liked that subject?"

You can also check in with a classmate if you are still connected and ask for his or her observations about your talents. Why ask someone who knew you in class? Because, as I always tell my coaching clients, "Life kicks in and we tend to forget the good things about ourselves – what comes naturally to us tends to be trumped by life's demands."

My favorite courses in school were history, English and music (sang in the school choir). These were my favorite teachers because they influenced me to reach high above my own expectations; they engaged me in the class. I remember telling my father that I wanted to be an anthropologist because of my history teacher. My love of writing came from the influence from my English teacher. I guess by now you know my love of performing – my music teacher made a huge impact by motivating me to play roles in the school plays.

Remembering a favorite teacher can help you rediscover your natural strengths and interests.

Remember

- If you cannot recall a favorite subject in school, think about what you did outside of school. Maybe a close relative introduced you to something that you loved to do or learned how to do.

- If you entertained yourself – what did you do that hours passed by and you enjoyed doing it. As an only child, until my brother came along when I was 12 (surprise!), I loved cutting out pictures of famous movie stars. This connects to my modeling and acting for TV and print commercials.

Funthentic Tip #12 – Learn Something New

"You have to do what you love to do, not get stuck in that comfort zone of a regular job. Life is not a dress rehearsal. This is it." Lucinda Basset

While consulting with an educational institution in Philadelphia, I met an 85-year-old man on the executive board who I will never forget. He was energetic and demonstrated an enormous quest for living. One day I asked him how he stayed so young at heart. "I learn something new every day," he said.

Learning something new helps to surface "silver star clues" about what you don't know or haven't yet discovered about your true self.

Remember my "Rounding Up the Old Crew" strategy? One of the comments from one of my high school friends when I rounded up my crew was how she remembered my love for acting in plays. That comment convinced me to enroll in an acting course at Freedom Theatre, in Philadelphia.

Taking an acting class was a difficult decision. It may not sound like a life-changing decision, but at that time in my life, I was dragging myself out of a hole of low self-esteem, experiencing a difficult divorce, and coping with being a single parent. I was afraid I would fail; however, I was determined to find a part of me I forgot. I wanted to experience the joy I felt in high school when I was performing.

I called the director of admissions, Tom Page, a friend of mine, and asked him if I could audition for the summer acting program. He was thrilled that I was pursuing my love of acting. We met and he gave me the monologue to rehearse for my audition. I was shocked when I read it. The character was a prostitute. I couldn't see myself memorizing the lines. Tom said that the monologue would challenge me to see if I really wanted to act.

While rehearsing for the audition I was terrified. I repeatedly phoned a friend to say, "I can't do this." She encouraged me to move through the fear. I knew that acting was a lost passion for me that needed rekindling. The last time I acted was in high school, and images of failure and humiliation filled my head.

I called Tom Page a week before the audition to cancel. His administrative assistant told me that Tom could not be reached and suggested that I show up for the audition. Little did I know at the time that Tom expected me to call and planned how to respond to my getting cold feet.

Tom told me during my initial meeting how he remembered that 15 years earlier, when my children were taking classes; I repeatedly would pop into his office and tell him how much I wanted to take an acting class. I used excuses of taking care of my daughters and how stressful my job was, requiring many hours during the week. I just could not find the time to squeeze the acting class in with my schedule. Tom would always smile and say, "That's fine. Let me know when you are ready."

Well, here I was, 15 years later - after a lot of procrastination and tears. I decided I had no choice. I prayed to God for courage in helping me to continue my path of self-discovery. I asked four close friends to help me practice for the audition. While reciting the words, I noticed how my friends focused on every word I was saying. I remember hearing my voice escalate at certain points in the monologue and found myself suddenly immersed in the words I was once afraid to recite. When I finished, my friends were astonished at how my voice and look changed once I got into character. They didn't understand my nervousness; they told me I was really good. Their votes of confidence sent me on my journey. It helps to have supportive friends when you are on this journey of finding your authenticity.

I went to the audition. Sitting next to young children waiting for my turn, I felt humbled. I kept thinking, "What if I forget the words?" I remembered a powerful quote, "Feel the fear and do it anyway.[2]"

I nervously recited my monologue before several acting instructors. It was not perfect, but I did it. To be honest, I rather enjoyed it. And, I was accepted into the course. I was excited to get over the first hurdle toward my goal.

I met interesting and creative people in the acting class. It was held three nights per week, with long hours rehearsing. The time felt endless as I rediscovered a joy suppressed from my past. Learning to act was thrilling.

The acting experience wasn't at all like spelunking, but it sure felt like it. I confronted my fear and received good grades for my final monologue. The renewed self-confidence was thrilling. I learned more about the real me. I found new skills that were buried for many years. Taking the classes felt therapeutic. The fear of trying something out of my comfort zone was real, but I did it anyway and moved through my archaeological dig in discovering the real me.

I feel fortunate that my "Rounding Up The Crew" dinner surfaced these wonderful memories because with a renewed sense of self-confidence and newfound information about me, I persisted with my journey of self-discovery. I continued taking acting lessons.

---

[2] Susan Jeffers, 1988

A few years later, my daughter, Monique, and my friend, Kimberly, spurred me to take the next step. They encouraged me to get involved in television commercials and print modeling. I was flattered, but apprehensive. "At my age?" I asked.

My daughter saw an opportunity for me to apply my love of performing as another layer in my career journey, and I was ready for the challenge.

Someone once told me that when you are navigating uncharted territory, the first step is the most difficult one. I did not know where to begin. Because my daughter and Kimberly were both involved in acting, they were my support coaches guiding me along the way. Les Brown has said, "When you need faith in yourself, just ride on someone else's faith in you." So, I rode on Monique's and Kimberly's faith during each step in my new "Learning Something New" experience.

I made an appointment with a photographer to have headshots taken for my portfolio. The next step was presenting my portfolio to various casting agents.

Following several interviews, three casting agents accepted me as a client. My first casting call found me among many other aspiring actors. I waited patiently for my turn to be interviewed by an advertising agency. As my name was called, I nervously entered the room. The agents sat in a row; all dressed in black, looking like stereotypical New Yorkers. One agent said, "Just tell us who you are."

It was interesting he said that considering I was already on my own quest to find out who I was.

I gave them my best description of me, and when I mentioned my age, they looked shocked. The agents gave me kudos for looking so great at my age with two young-adult daughters.

My first audition left me feeling positive about myself. I thought I did well. But I knew from my classes that it was best not to project overconfidence in the competitive entertainment industry. The advice I received was to pat myself on the back and move on to the next audition.

Surprisingly, my agent called me the next day and said that I booked my first national print ad. I did not know what the word "booking" meant. She explained that it meant I got the job. My mouth fell open. The job was to model an older healthy woman who appears to take risks. I was representing a national well-known athletic shoe company, and the creative art director mentioned that my picture would appear in all the brand's stores across the country.

I did not realize the impact of the ad until one day while walking in a shopping mall. I wasn't looking for the ad, but there it was smack in front of me in a full billboard in the store. After the initial shock, I went in the store and asked if I could have an extra copy. They were excited to see the real person in the ad show up in their store, and I tasted fame for a few minutes. I must admit it felt good. They gave me a copy of the picture and sample promotion boxes. What a thrill this was for me. Thanks to my daughter and Kimberly for believing in me and helping me to "Go fetch."

I continue auditioning and, fortunately, I have appeared in several movies, print and television spots. Currently, I book print ads for major advertising agencies. None of this would have happened if I had not taken a risk and made something happen in my life.

Changing Careers – From Teaching Elementary School to Counsel Adults Returning to School in Higher Education Administration

I took a risk and left teaching in elementary school to work as a supervisor for pre-admission counseling in Continuing Education for Women at Temple University in Philadelphia during the early 1970s. I counseled almost 400 women in one year who were returning to college after a long separation from education. Rewarding experiences came from watching women challenge themselves to rekindle their educational goals. One 70-year-old woman who came to my office for pre-admission counseling shared her experiences and passion for learning. It was so rewarding to hear. Her age was not a barrier, for she had a passion for learning. She believed that in another 10 years, she could accomplish her dream in pursuing an undergraduate degree.

Her energy was contagious. Many times when I was feeling drained at the end of a long day; she would bounce into my office sharing words of wisdom she learned in one of her new courses. She did accomplish her dream and graduated with an undergraduate degree. Several years ago, she left this life fulfilling her role as a minister and advocate, helping people to fulfill their dreams. Before she passed away, I asked her what she discovered about herself when returning to school after such a long time. She told me that she realized her brain was not old; it could still take in new information. She proved that learning never stops, and with faith, you can achieve anything in life.

Many of those women I counseled completed challenging goals filled with obstacles. They had small children to look after, husbands who complained about their wives taking time away from home, and were working at full-time jobs. They moved forward determined to learn something new. These women uncovered the hidden gems deep inside that were buried for many years. This position was an important step in creating a work history to prove I can work in adult learning. Later on in my career this work experience led to my being hired in a corporate setting. My natural talent to coach and counsel adults surfaced at Temple University.

You, too, may be struggling to find the courage to participate in a career empowerment activity. Round up friends who will support you on your quest and who will not allow you to give up. Ride into the fear.

What is it you want to learn? New learning means taking part in something you enjoy. Has someone reminded you of something you liked doing? The secret to succeeding in learning something new is to remember what Anthony Robbins says, "There are no failures, only results." Only after learning something new will you discover new gems inside yourself.

There are no guarantees as to what you'll discover. You may find out you don't like the new activity, and that's OK. It can transition you through a process of elimination.

I took a photography class once, and it did not work for me. Was this wasted time? No, it gave me new information about myself, and I learned something new in the meantime. To this day, my family does not count on me to be the photographer at family events. Don't beat yourself up if your activity does not work. Just keep moving and "Go fetch it" some more.

Remember

- "There is no such thing as failure, only results", says Tony Robbins. Whatever you decide to learn, you will not fail; you will discover something new you never learned before.

- Learning something new keeps the brain cells working and slows down the aging process.

- Create a safety zone when fear creeps in – mine was my therapist; your safety net may be faith, a best friend, a spouse or significant other.

Funthentic Tip #13 – Create Your Own Personal Board of Directors

"Discovering Your Authentic Self" is Chapter 2 in my book, *"It's Your Turn: Find Your Authentic Self and Go Fetch It!"* This chapter identifies four activities that help you to look inward to find hidden talents and gifts: (1) Return to the past, (2) Round up the old crew, (3) Meet one-on-one, and (4) Get out of your comfort zone and learn something new.

These activities are helpful in finding your true self. Some participants in my "It's Your Turn" seminars find these activities challenging. Concerns range from "I am retiring at 60, but feel like I am 40 – now what do I do with my life?" to "I need motivation to redefine who I am" to "Defining my authentic self feels like work and it is time consuming" or "I need to work – how can I plan my next career while I am working?" and "I know how to do a lot of things, and I feel frustrated that I must select one interest – which one do I choose to be my life's work?" or even, "I don't have the energy to change." All of these responses are valid and real. Looking inside ourselves is no easy task, but benefits are far more rewarding when you discover you are more than you think you are.

How can looking inward to find hidden talents and gifts feel less challenging and fearful? Asking people for support as you rediscover yourself is a conscious effort to help you achieve your goal.

Let's call this group of people your "Personal Board of Directors" (PBOD). Your PBOD should be made up of individuals that play a significant role in helping you rediscover your hidden talents and gifts. A PBOD offers advice, knowledge, or support on your journey to your authentic self. Your PBOD may include close friends, family members, or professionals that genuinely want the best for you.

I began creating my PBOD when both of my daughters were in college at the same time. With them gone, I felt like parts of me were missing. Wondering how to cope with the empty nest syndrome, I decided to call a close friend. Tearfully, I said, "I miss my babies." Only a mother could have flashbacks of their adult children as "babies" in her arms. My friend responded, "Well maybe it's now time for you to grow." I recall how I was taken aback by this statement. "Maybe it's time for me to grow?" The word "grow" was confusing at the time. I thought, being an adult, my growing was completed. After our conversation, I wanted to learn more about "growing" as an adult. There weren't many talk shows like "The Oprah Winfrey Show" or many self-help books in the mid-1980s. I found two books that changed my life, Dr. Wayne Dyer's book "*Pulling Your Own Strings*" and Dr. M. Scott Peck's book, *"The Road Less Traveled."* Both books motivated me to continue my quest to find out who I am. I found the courage to seek therapy to help me cope with issues of fear in finding the true me. I found a wonderful therapist who was compassionate, but firm. She helped me unpeel the layers of shame and pain needed to begin on my archaeological dig to rediscover me. One of my first tasks in therapy was to buy flowers for myself. I went to flower shop, nervously picking out beautiful flowers that made me smile. This may seem like a simple act, but the roles of a mother and a wife distracted me from taking the time to love me. Buying me flowers was a conscious and deliberate act of doing the work to find me. I like this quote by Dolly Parton, "The way I see it, if you want the rainbow, you gotta put up with the rain." Find out who you are and do it on purpose.

Therapy may not be the support you need or feel comfortable with to discover your authentic self. Select a close friend best suited for your journey. A close friend is someone you trust, love, who will not be judgmental when you make your request for support.

As I continued on my journey to find my true self, I discovered my passion to teach. I did not want to remain in the corporate environment all my life. I decided to prepare to teach in academia and enroll in a terminal degree program while working as a manager of training in a major health care organization. I selected two of my closest friends to be part of my PBOD. Eugena's role was to call me every day while working on my dissertation to make sure I completed eight pages each day. She played an important role because it was helpful to be accountable to someone. My friend, Janet, would call me to make sure I ate dinner out at least once per week to reward my writing accomplishments. Both of my friends were valuable in supporting me to achieve my goal to return to school.

Selecting a friend as a coach could be another member of your PBOD. One of the benefits in my rediscovery process was remembering I enjoyed participating in sports and feeling my body move. I realized I wanted to return to those feelings again.

To help me recapture the healthy lifestyle, I selected my friend, Darlene, to be part of my PBOD. Darlene was a physical fitness guru and was actively involved in exercise. She agreed to support me in getting to the gym three times per week. This was no easy task, but we set up a commitment agreement for three months. Darlene convinced me that fulfilling the three-month commitment would create the benefits of feeling good. I am now addicted to working out because the benefit of feeling good after a good workout is a wonderful feeling, and more importantly, being active is who I am.

These are just a few examples of people who became members of my PBOD. When you embark on the journey of finding your true self the universe says "yes" to you. Watch who supports you on your self-discovery journey. Surround yourself with people who provide what you need to get through the rediscovery. Women, especially, often subscribe to the "super woman" syndrome, thinking "I can do this alone" or asking "Why should someone want to help me?" Rubbish! Ask someone you care about or who cares about you and listen to his or her response.

If you find that reaching out to people is a challenge, then try to widen your scope and reach out through networking. Once you make the decision to find out more about you, networking provides opportunities for people to show up for you and provide support as you move through your journey.

Today, my PBOD has increased to include attorneys, a business coach, an accountant, even doctors, since good health is an important issue as we get older.

There is a hidden talent in you – Like the "Sankofa" bird, return to the past and build a future.

I was desperate to fill this empty void inside of me that was yearning to feel whole and complete. Embarking on my journey created an overwhelming fear of the unknown, especially since I was experiencing a difficult divorce and the challenges of being a single mother. The first step of my journey was to seek support. I was unaware at the time that this was the beginning of creating a support team that later became my "personal board of directors."

Having a support team keeps you humble and grateful. You know at some graduations they ask the people to stand up who helped this person to achieve. Visualize your support team with a standing ovation. Here I am!!! I was on the team!!

Remember

- You deserve support on your journey to self-discovery.

- Your close friends want to help you.

- You are not an expert in everything you know. There are people who know more than you do.

- Let go and let people enjoy your ride of curiosity.

Funthentic Tip # 14 – Visualize Your Authentic Life

Discovering my authentic self was a revelation of new feelings and new thoughts about who I really am. Gathering information about my true self, I realized that I am more than I thought I was. I began to feel and see myself in ways that felt true to me. I used all the "silver star" clues of information I discovered about me and began thinking about creating a purposeful life that is filled with joy and feeling congruent with the fluidity of moving through life with ease and doing things that are truly who I am.

Visualization is a technique I discovered reading a book by Dr. Maxwell Maltz called "*Psycho-Cybernetic Principles for Creative Living.*" The word "cybernetics" comes from a Greek word that means "steersman." Servo-mechanisms are constructed that they automatically "steer" their way to a goal, target or "answer." Dr. Maltz states that the brain is like a maze. When we set the vision, the brain begins to find the end result. As the brain begins to do its work, you will meet people or receive the information you need to complete your vision. Our brain and nervous system acts as a goal-striving mechanism that operates automatically to achieve a certain goal. Dr. Maltz calls this goal-striving mechanism a "servo-mechanism" which we use and operates like an electronic computer or a guidance system. Dr. Maltz clearly points out that he is not saying we are "machines," rather we have a machine that we use – the human brain.

Now that you have a new image of your authentic self, there has to be a reason for embracing your new authentic self. I use Dr. Maltz's theory of visualization based on "truth" of who I really am. I began to see and feel who I really am.

I love Dr. Maltz's belief that science has now confirmed what philosophers, mystics, and other intuitive people have long declared: Every human being has been literally "engineered for success" by his Creator. Every human being has access to a power greater than himself. This means YOU.

Imagine yourself doing and feeling your authentic self – all the things you discovered on your journey is you. Having a goal to achieve one thing that you do with ease is a beginning to creating a vision for yourself. Your goal can be small or something bigger than you. The goal has to be something that is already happening now – almost like claiming that it is beginning as you set the goal. I love this because this connects to affirming and believing that it is already happening. Once you ask the question or create the target, the brain and the universe start to move you toward receiving what you asked for.

Think in terms of the end result – this is important because the brain supplies the means, and you supply the goal. The universe takes care of everything in between.

As you move through this visioning and goal-setting, you will hit bumps in your journey – don't be discouraged. Keep moving forward. I believe this is the only way you can achieve your goal, by learning what works and what doesn't work. The brain is like a maze – picture a mouse running around trying to get to the cheese at the end. What happens – he hits walls and then keeps going to reach that cheese, and he does reach it. Well, that's what happens when you reach your target goal.

I used Dr. Maltz's theory to create my authentic careers that I describe in my previous book. I have four vision boards in my home. I cut out pictures using the information I discovered about my true self – Health, Spirituality, Abundance, and Creativity. These were the areas that I wanted to focus on moving forward. Your areas may be different, depending on your authentic discovery.

Remember

- Pull together all the information you gathered in "Discovering Your Authenticity"
- Visualize every detail of the career.
- Cut out pictures and place them on a board or in a picture album.
- Look at the pictures frequently or put them in a location that is in your line of vision.
- State your intention through prayer, affirmation, or meditation.
- Claim your divine inheritance of abundance.

OK, now you've done the work and are ready for growing the new you. The process of growing into your authentic self is relevant to your own journey. No one can predict how long it will take you to find the true you. But guess what? The good news is that "finding you" does happen. It happens incrementally – you will know when the light of finding you is gleaming. Growing the new you is a wonderful opportunity in your mid-life. Get it right, whatever that means to you.

These activities can lead you to discovering your natural strengths that can lead to creating funding streams.

Part III

"Find a way to get paid for doing what you love. Then every paycheck will be a bonus." Oprah Winfrey (excerpt from The Top 20 Things Oprah Knows for Sure).

Chapter 9 – Funding Streams

As we approach midlife or if you are in midlife trying to figure out how to make ends meet, multiple funding streams can increase your income.

By now, you've read how my life experiences helped me discover my authentic self. The "**Funthentic Tips**" were ways to discover my natural and hidden strengths. **Funthentic Tip #1**- I talked to close friends who reminded me of my love to perform – this led to being a mature model for TV and print. This money is not consistent – but it's a funding stream that increases my income. **Funthentic Tip #2** - I dialogued with a close friend who gave insight into my creativity – the outcome was I published my first book in 2006 – now in its fourth printing. Book signings became my second funding stream. I discovered a critical core value in **Funthentic Tip #3** that guides me in how I want to live my life. **Funthentic Tip #4** challenged me to experience my inner strength.

My funding streams were created by knowing that I am a powerful woman who doesn't need anyone to define who I am. When I stretch myself I need my inner power to take the next step to create another funding stream. I'm currently working on a major project that is a risk – but this tip helped be to focus on what I learned about myself as a leader.

Funthentic Tips 5-10 are resource tools that surface my natural strengths as a teacher and professional speaker. I wrote my life story, I went to therapy to help me remove barriers to discovering my strengths, I brainstorm ways to promote my book and speaking – many ideas surfaced some fear – but I did them anyway. As a result, I created a wonderful website with a talented, creative designer, Erin Hyland and business coach Karyn Greenstreet. I published several articles for two major magazines. My mission statement keeps me grounded and focused.

Funthentic Tip # 10 - I continue to pray and meditate – this is imperative to my ability to keep creating ways to live my life in gratitude for my funding streams. People that read my book and heard me speak asked for additional activities and I created **Funthentic Tips 11- 14.**

Funding streams is an easier way of what to do next in my third act of life. When you think of one way to increase your income you are limiting yourself. Look over your life – your experiences surfaced strengths and talents that can be turned into different funding streams. Try two tips and be open – maybe you want to try only one tip – this is a beginning. Be open to the possibility of a new you in many different ways.

"You take away from the world when you're not yourself. Whatever is unique and special about you was designed by God. And when you try to be someone else, we don't get you. Who knows what you would have contributed to the world had you just been yourself, if you just celebrated who you are and just walked boldly?"
Queen Latifah - Excerpted from an article about Queen Latifah in MORE magazine- 2012

Chapter 10 - Growing the New You

I heard a sermon given by the Rev. Sheila Pierce of the Center of Peace, a wonderful friend and spiritual teacher. Her topic was growing a new you and she used the metaphor of a lobster. "People should behave like lobsters," she says, "and spend their lives continually molting."

We have a lot to learn from a clawed creature that removes himself from his old shell in order to grow a new one dozens of times over, said the pastor on a recent Sunday at the Center of Peace in Philadelphia. Our inner growth process can change just as often in the search of our true self.

While a lobster prepares for molting, his old shell cracks and he backs out of it, leaving it behind. In the new soft shell, he is vulnerable to predators and must remain in hiding while waiting for his shell to harden.

The vulnerable membrane is at risk of hitting the coral, so he burrows to feel safe. After several weeks, the lobster has fully grown into its shell, and the cycle of molting and growing begins again.

Our own spiritual journeys to discover our hidden talents may follow a similar path. In doing so, we need to:

- Shed fears that hold back the courage to grow.

- Shed values that do not work anymore.

- Shed negative energy that blocks inner growth.

- Shed feeling like a victim. That inhibits the ability to feel empowered.

The lobster's path tells us that feeling vulnerable while growing is only natural. And, while we may be comfortable with our old selves because of our work, titles, and likes or dislikes, we must step out of these comfort zones. Just as the lobster burrows itself in a safe place while waiting for a new shell, we can regenerate in safe havens while transforming our lives, too.

Give yourself permission to take a "love me" break.

"I've done well," "I am super mom/superwoman," "The day is over, I am exhausted, but this a good thing" are affirmations I said as a busy mom working long hours and feeling exhausted at the end of a busy day. Little did I realize that these affirmations were a setup for a false premise on what it meant to love me. I was looking through the wrong lens of what loving me looks like. In a way, I had it backwards – loving me from the outside instead of the inside.

Being on automatic pilot sometimes comes with the role and responsibility of parenting. Attending school activities and organizing play-dates that the work schedule will allow are important in raising children. Transporting children to activities is a way of life for many moms. Where does loving me fit into the daily routine of being a mom? Working long hours, striving to reach the top of the corporate ladder – feeling burnt out and wondering is this all I have may be barriers to taking care of you. Whatever leaves you feeling physically and emotionally spent are warning signs that "self" needs your attention.

Discovering your authentic love of self begins with giving yourself permission to say, "It's my turn," even if it is only for a few minutes out of the busy day. Taking a break probably feels like a luxury. However, the outcome of avoiding "loving me" time aborts the process of connecting to self and maintaining a healthy mind and body.

When the body continues on automatic pilot over a long period of time — without a "love me" break or acknowledging the inner good — the body and/or mind suffers. The body will continually send out red flag messages and physical warnings crying out for attention. The result of not paying attention to physical and mental needs while taking care of the family is a high cost to pay and the body will shut down. Setting aside "love me" time is like taking a mental break acknowledging the feeling of being a good mom. This is who I am: loving, kind, or whatever affirmation offers feelings of inner love.

Taking a few minutes during the day to treat yourself is an opportunity to focus on who you are and what makes you the person you are. This precious "loving me" time could be reading an inspiring passage out of your favorite book that sits somewhere close by, or gazing out the window and reflecting on your gratitude that day. One of the greatest benefits of taking a "love me" break is that present moment brings you back to self, even for a few minutes.

"The answers will come when you trust your inner spirit and believe that your life is divinely guided." Dr. Barbara Collins – Writer, Speaker and Professor

Chapter 11 – Conclusion

I'm excited about completing my second book, *"Power in Midlife and Beyond: 14 "Funthentic" Ways to Live an Authentic Life, speak your truth, create a second career and increase income being the real you."* When I called my editor to discuss next steps, she mentioned, "Barbara you haven't completed your conclusion." Surprisingly, I forgot about the conclusion. I was focused on completing the last chapter. I was anxious to meet the deadline to complete the book.

Rebirthing the book continues; it's like baking this wonderful cake perfecting the outcome and you realize the cake looks wonderful but it's not done. What? I said to myself, "Are you kidding me?" There is a reason why it's not done yet. I know why – a surprise was waiting for me.

I reread my entire manuscript to get into the flow for writing the conclusion. Reading the entire manuscript after a long time was an awakening for me; the content reminded me of why I wrote this book in the first place. Ok, enough reflecting, I digress. Truthfully, I think I was procrastinating to write the conclusion. First, I hope you enjoyed reading the sequel to my first book – *It's Your Turn Find Your Authentic Self and Go Fetch It!* For many weeks, what to say stayed with me – until I made a startling discovery.

One evening, while sitting in my office going through an old file, several pieces of paper fell on the floor. On the papers were notes and quotations written almost five years ago when I attended an art and spirituality workshop. I looked at the papers and wondered what was going on in my life when I wrote these words? Is this a poem? Were these words answering a question in the workshop? Did the facilitator give us a task? I slowly read each word and wondered did I really write these words? Of course I did because the words described who I am. Yes, it is a poem. As I continued reading the poem the words were a culmination of my work. I thought, "I did discover my authentic self," because I did the work. I'm still discovering my natural strengths, but finding this poem was a powerful awareness that I want to share in the conclusion.

My poem was revealed at the right time to write my conclusion. Answers to life questions typically lay dormant to be revealed at the right time. When you are ready to listen the teacher appears. I want my readers to know that self-discovery does happen. You never know the place or time when information about who you are comes together, but it does. I discovered who I am doing my own "funthentic" tips. I discovered in the poem what comes natural to me; my creativity, my inner spirit that speaks to me every day, every moment to remind me who I am and why I'm here and what I need to do. I discovered that my ancestors passed down natural strengths to me. Understanding connections and experiences in my life were layers of self -discovery.

I did all the "funthentic" exercises that are in this book. Not all at once, I made up the tips when more information was needed to discover my authentic self. I just said let's go see, let's experiment. The exercises helped me to write the poem. My discovery surfaced as a poem in the arts and spirituality workshop. Rediscovering my natural strengths and affirming that I now see that I am worth the work was exhilarating. I probably couldn't have written the poem without these activities. Finding the poem was like receiving a gift.

Your discovery about who you are may surface in a different form. Maybe a book you read will give clarity to your authentic work. Your authentic work may come together while sharing your authentic discovery with a friend or loved one. Knowing that your authentic discovery will happen is exciting. I don't know how your authentic journey will show up because our journeys take on different paths. Remember I described how Dr. Maxwell Maltz's theory about the brain is like a maze? When you set the goal, the brain finds its way. I found my way. You will find your way, trust me.

"Funthentic" tips are fun, some of the tips may feel a little daunting at first but you can do them. The natural gifts and talents that God gave you to bring in this world were not accidents. This is your DNA. I learned that God has a plan for our lives. All of what I learned about what comes easy to me was always inside of me. I just had to scrape off the layers of life's distractions and find my way to the core of me.

Living authentically in midlife and beyond can be a way to increase your income, work authentically and communicate with authentic power in midlife. My hope for you is to be in your own skin at all times. As we get older there is no time to waste living a false life. I want you to live a truthful life. Be at peace with the master plan. No need to spend time being what someone thinks you should be. There is enough for you to do just being you. I have post-its® all over my house to remind me every day to ask, "What Do I Want To Do"? Now I can answer this question comfortably because there is evidence about who I am. Some days are harder than others to think about what I want to do. But you know the difference for me now is when I ask the question I know I deserve to think about the answer. Doesn't that give you a good feeling? In midlife it feels wonderful to respond, "no not now, no I prefer to think about it, .no this is not working for me." I'm sure there are plenty of yes's that feel authentic, but saying "no" takes practice.

Many women ask me how long will it take to find your authentic self. It takes as long as your life journey doesn't need to ask the question of who I am any more. You will know. The journey to discovering the real you is like walking in a dark tunnel or a long road with no end in sight. Then all of a sudden a flicker of light appears when you discovered something new about you. The light of self-awareness gets brighter and brighter when you keep discovering more about who you are.

I was sitting at my dinner table reading an article in *Ebony Magazine* about New York City, where I was born. All of a sudden, I had a flash back of the things I loved to do while growing up in the Bronx. I recalled how I loved to go to Manhattan Center and the Palladium with my cousin to enjoy Salsa dancing. I smiled, yes, that's who I am. My memories could hear the music, see the dance steps. I was in my skin of who I am. It's never too late to do what comes easy in midlife. Joyful feelings return. Maybe Salsa dancing all night is not realistic right now. But, I can enjoy Salsa with a few moves I still remember. My bright light just got bigger. There's a smile on my face.

Here is my poem. There is no title. Happy authentic journey...

Waking to me

Who am I?

Waking to me

Who Am I?

My Spirit tugs at me.

My Ancestors sing,

Orators, play instruments,

Ministers, writers, teachers and artists.

I see beautiful colors surround me

When I think about who I am here's what I say.

Who Am I?

Yes, to my creativity.

Yes, to my love of Salsa

Yes, to my Caribbean history and dancing moves.

Yes, to my love of theatre and acting

Yes, to my Inner Spirit.

Yes, I'm a child of God.

Yes, I'm aware of my body – oh so aware –

sometimes feeling everything is exhausting –

but I know God helps me use this for good.

Yes, to the first time I spoke to a large audience

at "Camp Miniwanca." (a magical place)

Yes, to Center for Peace

Yes, to my gift of teaching – so Blessed

Yes, to Oceans/Peaceful

I'm here – I know who I am.

What a Blessing!

The journey still goes on.

I give you permission to reflect on your journey!!!

Let me know what you discovered.

Peace and Blessings…

About the Author

Dr. Barbara R. Collins, management development consultant, executive coach, professor, keynote speaker and author, began her career as an educator. She started as an elementary school teacher in Philadelphia, PA teaching fourth grade and later becoming a high school guidance counselor. Barbara was passionate about teaching and working with students.

However, as a divorced and single parent, she left education to increase her income. Barbara entered the corporate world as a human resources development manager at Independence Blue Cross in Philadelphia, where during her 11 years she designed and implemented training programs for more than 1,400 employees. Barbara later was employed as an organizational development internal consultant, assisting in the Corporate Wide, Total Quality and Diversity Culture Change initiative at Core States Financial, also in Philadelphia.

Barbara's parents instilled in her the importance of education at an early age. She received her Bachelor's Degree in Elementary Education from Cheyney State University, in Cheyney, PA, and Master's Degree in Education, specializing in Counseling Psychology, from Antioch University, in Yellow Springs, OH, and her Doctorate in Group and Organizational Behavior from Temple University in Philadelphia.

During Barbara's 20-plus years in business, she created her own consulting company, Positive Trends, Inc., which specializes in helping organizations develop and implement strategic initiatives to enhance work productivity and achieve organizational goals. Barbara helped numerous clients maximize people differences to accomplish business goals, manage change in a changing environment, and learn effective team group process strategies. Barbara's clients have included the Philadelphia Department of Public Health, Philadelphia Water Department, University of Pennsylvania Health System, New York State Council on the Arts, PECO Energy, Philadelphia School District, Pennsylvania Convention Center and numerous others. Her keynote presentations have been given to the 11th Annual CITR Conference, Consortium of Information and Telecommunications Executives, Inc., Bell Atlantic, School District of Philadelphia, POWA (Professional Women of Antigua-Barbuda), Women in Transportation Services, Jack and Jill, Inc.-Philadelphia Chapter and many more.

While working in education and business, Barbara began her journey of self-discovery. Today, Barbara's life has transformed from what she had to do into doing what she loves and what feels authentically right. She is working in her dharma, a feeling of timelessness. Her inner search during the past 20 years has taken her on a wonderful and exciting journey of self-discovery that finds her a TV and print commercial actor, associate professor, professional keynote speaker and executive life coach.

Today, she dedicates her work to helping women find their authentic self. Barbara realized many years ago that finding our Divine purpose takes work and proactive planning; it doesn't just happen or fall into our laps. Her first book, It's Your Turn: Find Your Authentic Self and Go Fetch It! presents activities that help women discover natural strengths to create second and third careers. Her keynote presentations "It's Your Turn" and "You're More Than You Think You Are" are praised by numerous organizations.

Clients – Cabrini College, Rosemont College, Widener University and Main Line Health were well received by Women's Leadership Forums. Client Vertex,

Inc., I look forward to hearing her powerful presentation "Discovering Your Authentic Leadership."

To help Barbara proactively build her new career as a keynote speaker and coach, she created her own personal board of directors. Barbara incorporates a synergistic approach to remain authentic in working with women. H.G. Chissel, well known Feng Shui consultant, along with Ginni Stiles, professional organizer, helped Barbara to be clear about her intentions both in her personal and professional life, and assisted her in building an organized infrastructure. Barbara's award-winning web designer, David Kaneda, was part of her team to ensure that the communication to women is congruent with the goals in building the foundation for "It's Your Turn." Today Erin Hyland, web designer and administrator, continues to maintain Barbara's web site.

As an active member, currently her memberships include The Society, Inc., a non-profit organization that promotes youth in the arts, and Alpha Kappa Alpha, Inc.

For more information about Dr. Collins, please contact:

Dr. Barbara R. Collins
Positive Trends, Inc.
P.O. Box 26181
Collegeville, PA 19426
Voice: 610-409-8905
Fax: 610-409-8902
www.drbarbaracollins.com
keynote@drbarbaracollins.com

Dr. Barbara R. Collins
Positive Trends, Inc.
P.O. Box 26181
Collegeville, PA 19426
Voice: 610-409-8905
Fax: 610-409-8902
www.drbarbaracollins.com
keynote@drbarbaracollins.com

CPSIA information can be obtained
at www.ICGtesting.com
Printed in the USA
BVHW042335230419
546356BV00005B/6/P

9 781495 104541